25 KIDS
WHO CHANGED
AMERICAN HISTORY

SHORT, INSPIRING BIOGRAPHIES WITH
ILLUSTRATIONS AND DISCUSSION GUIDES
FOR YOUNG READERS

N. H. GREENWOOD

SAGE VI PRESS

"THE BEST WAY TO PREDICT YOUR FUTURE
IS TO CREATE IT."

—ABRAHAM LINCOLN, 16TH U.S. PRESIDENT

CONTENTS

INTRODUCTION

On a dark, rainy evening in 1777, a sixteen-year-old girl named Sybil Ludington leaped onto her horse and rode 40 miles alone through the night. Her family and neighbors were counting on her. It was the American Revolution, and enemy soldiers were everywhere. Sybil rode across villages and farms to warn American forces that an attack was coming. Her brave ride helped gather enough soldiers to fight off the British.

Sybil's message didn't just help save her hometown – it helped change history. And she was just a teenager! Pretty incredible, right?

I wrote this book to share stories like Sybil's – stories of young people who made a real impact on American history, often before they even turned 20. I wanted today's kids to understand that the America we live in was shaped by actual kids throughout history, young people who faced challenges, stood up for what they believed in, and made a difference. History is about people just like you!

What's in this Book. Here's what I think makes this the right book for you. First, the chapters all have graphic-novel-style illustrations that make the stories more fun and easier to imagine. A word about those pictures – they are not meant to be *exactly* what people and places looked like but to give you a close idea as you learn about these amazing events.

Then, after each biography, you will find a discussion guide with review questions to check on what you've read, discussion questions to think about the big lessons the story touches, and project ideas to do something fun after reading. These features will help bring history to life and let you dive deeper into the stories.

Big Events. But this book is not just about the stories! You will also read about different periods and events in American history as you read about the kids. Everything is split into groups of biographies. You will hear about young heroes from the 13 Colonies, the American Revolution, the move westward, the Civil War, the Industrial Revolution, the Civil Rights Movement, the Cold War and more. Each biography combines personal tales with historical context, so you can learn about U.S. history and also understand why these kids mattered to the bigger story of America.

Who Are the 25 Kids. Let's talk about how I chose these 25 kids. I looked for young people who made real contributions while they were teenagers or younger. They were active in lots of fields, from military to sports, arts to science. I wanted to include boys and girls from different backgrounds, regions and perspectives. This book is focused on action, impact and citizenship – it is not political.

I trust most of these kids will be new to you. You may have already heard of some of them as some did go on to become very famous, but they were chosen only if they started on their path to fame when they were young. Either way, I know you're going to love them!

About the Author. Let me share a bit about myself. I'm N. H. Greenwood, an Ivy League history graduate and lawyer, and I have three kids of my own. My heart for U.S. history started when I was young. To raise money for charity, I rode my bicycle across America in college. I discovered that American history means something different to everyone, and it is inspiring everywhere. New Englanders get excited about the Revolution. Westerners love the legends of the frontier.

About You! So, I want to make sure all young people get a chance to be inspired by history. I believe my children will be happier, more productive citizens – better neighbors and even better people – if they understand the American civilization they're part of and where it comes from. I also think it helps to see how so many of these kids found passions at a young age and bravely shaped their futures – and America's!.. But more on these lessons at the end of the book.

Overall. By reading these biographies, you can expect to learn about history in a fun way. You'll discover the courage, creativity, and hard work of kids who helped make this country. You'll also learn about the times they lived in, including big events from the Salem Witch Trials to the Miracle on Ice. You'll see that you don't have to be a grownup to do something special.

So let's begin this journey through time. Let's meet these young heroes. And who knows? Someday, someone might write about the awesome things you did as a kid. History is waiting!

PART I

☆ ☆ ☆

FASCINATING KIDS OF THE COLONIES

CHAPTER 1

MARY CHILTON (1607-1679)

THE FIRST PILGRIM GIRL TO STEP ASHORE

The first European female to set foot in New England was just 13 years old. Her name was Mary Chilton. It was 1620. She didn't wait for a grown-up to go first. She was so excited to brave the New World that she got off the boat, ran up the beach and jumped up on Plymouth Rock before the others! Her courage inspired her fellow Pilgrims, and her legend lives on in Massachusetts today. Let's hear more.

The Mayflower left England for America in September 1620. The ship carried 102 passengers, many known as the Pilgrims, who were searching for a new home where they could practice their religion freely. Mary Chilton was only 13 years old when she boarded the boat with her parents. The journey across the Atlantic Ocean was long and hard. The Mayflower was crowded. There was little food, and the passengers often felt sick. Storms tossed the ship around, making the voyage even more frightening.

After more than two months at sea, the Mayflower finally saw land in November 1620. The passengers were relieved but also nervous. They had hoped to land in Virginia but were far north of that, where it was colder and lesser known. They dropped their anchor in what is now Provincetown Harbor, Massachusetts.

Mary Chilton's moment came on December 21, 1620. The Pilgrims decided to explore Plymouth Harbor, and legend says that Mary was so eager that she became the first European female to jump onto Plymouth Rock. Stepping onto solid ground after months at sea must have been both thrilling and scary.

As the first Pilgrim girl to set foot on the new land, Mary's actions meant hope and new beginnings. But right away, she and her family faced many challenges in the new colony. Life in the early days of Plymouth was tough, especially for the children. Like other kids, Mary had to help cook and clean, fetch water, and gather firewood. There weren't any schools, so children learned life skills from their parents. They had to grow up quickly and take on jobs that would be hard for kids today to imagine. The first winter was brutal, and nearly half of the Pilgrims died from cold, hunger, and disease. Mary's mother was one of those who died, and Mary and her father had to rely on the support of the others to survive.

Despite the hardships, Mary and the other Pilgrims worked hard to establish their new town. They built houses, planted seeds, and made peace with the Native Americans. The Wampanoag tribe helped the Pilgrims learn how to grow corn and other crops. This cooperation was vital for the survival of the colony.

The Pilgrims' story is a story of determination and community teamwork. The Pilgrims left England because they wanted religious freedom. They were willing to face the wilderness of the New World to worship as they chose. Cold, death and hunger would not stop them. They had a strong faith in the path they were on and would not give up.

They also kept their promises to each other. Remember, they had planned to arrive in America in Virginia near other colonists who were already there. But when they landed north of there in Plymouth, they found themselves on their own. They had to make their own rules. So the Pilgrims signed the Mayflower Compact, which was an agreement to create fair laws for their new village and to work together for the common good. Over time, the Compact showed they could run things without a king. It was the first step toward self-government in the New World.

You can see how the Pilgrims' success was due to their hard work and their ability to form strong bonds with each other and the Native Americans. Today, schools and history books tell this powerful tale of the Pilgrims, and even among these stories Mary Chilton's courage is remembered – a private club is still named for her in Boston! Young Mary's bold first step continues to inspire people to face challenges head-on 400 years later.

DISCUSSION GUIDE

Review Questions:

1. What was the name of the Pilgrim's ship? Where did it leave from?

2. Where did the Pilgrims plan to land, and where did they actually land in the New World?

3. What was the agreement that the Pilgrims signed, and what did it mean?

Discussion Questions:

1. Mary's journey on the Mayflower was long, uncomfortable, and dangerous, but she and her family took the risk for a better life. Have you ever done something scary or challenging because you believed it would lead to something better? How did it turn out?

2. If you could only pack three things for a big move, what

would you bring?

3. When Mary got off the boat, she was in a totally new place. How would you feel if you had to leave your home and move to a new, unknown place?

4. What would you do for fun without sports, TVs or toys?

Project Idea:

Ask your parents for permission first. Pilgrim children often helped with cooking. Choose a Pilgrim recipe such as Stewed Pumpkin or Boiled bread. Find one you're excited about online, and prepare it for a pretend Plymouth meal. Here's a simple recipe for Pilgrim-style *stewed pumpkin.*

Ingredients: 2 cups fresh pumpkin, peeled and diced (butternut squash as substitute); 1 cup milk; 1 tbsp butter; 1 1/2 tbsp maple syrup; 1/4 tsp salt; 1/2 tsp cinnamon

Directions:
1. **Check with your parents**; simmer diced pumpkin and milk in pot over medium heat, stirring in milk
2. Bring pumpkin and milk to light simmer, then reduce to low heat
3. Cook for 20-30 minutes, stirring occasionally until pumpkin is soft
4. Stir in butter, maple syrup, salt and cinnamon
5. Cook about 5 more minutes, mashing with a spoon until thick and stewed
6. Serve warm as side dish or spread on bread, just like Mary Chilton would have!

Chapter 2

Ann Putnam (1679-1716)

Regret in Salem

*I*n 1691, at the tender age of twelve, Ann Putnam found herself at the center of a panic – an out-of-control fear – that would change her community forever. Ann was one of the girls who said her neighbors were witches in Salem, Massachusetts. Those claims led to a wave of alarm and punishment for the so-called witches. This role does not make Ann a hero at all. Still, she is in this book to show the impact that even kids' bad behavior can have, and also because years later, Ann would be the only accuser who made a public apology for what she'd done! Not quite heroic but apologies take courage. Ann's story shows how saying you're sorry can help everyone heal, including yourself.

Ann Putnam was the oldest of ten children born into a prominent family in Salem, Massachusetts. Her father, Thomas Putnam, was a sergeant in the local militia and a well-known man in the community. The Putnam family had their share of arguments with other villagers, and those fights may have made Ann want to get revenge on certain people during the witch trials.

In the winter of 1691, Ann and a group of other young girls began experiencing strange fits and seizures - uncontrolled body movements. They claimed to see and feel evil spirits. A local doctor, unable to find a medical explanation for their illness, said that the girls were being attacked by witches. This idea set off a rush of confusion and fear. Ann, along with the other cursed girls, started accusing different members of the community of witchcraft. Ann's father, Thomas, supported these accusations and helped get the authorities involved on behalf of the girls.

What Ann said about the accused witches - her testimony – played a big part in creating the panic that gripped Salem. She accused a total of 62 people of witchcraft, leading to the execution (killing) of 18. Her accusations were often based on "spectral evidence," which meant she said she saw the accused doing witchcraft in her dreams and in her head but not in real life. This type of evidence was not trustworthy but was still allowed by the court. In the end, Ann's lies had terrible consequences. Innocent people were accused, imprisoned, and even put to death—all because of something that wasn't true.

Years later, in 1706, Ann did something unexpected. She stood before her church and admitted she had been wrong. She made a public apology for the role she played in the witch trials, saying she had been deceived by the devil. She expressed deep regret for the harm she caused, admitting the awful mistakes of the past. Ann was the only one of the accusers to offer such an apology. Her show of regret was important because it helped everyone admit that the trials were harmful. The apology healed some of the wounds left by the tragic events.

The Salem witch trials resulted from the times in which the colonists lived. The Puritans, who settled in Massachusetts, were very religious people. They believed that the devil was always looking for ways to trick them. This belief made them suspicious (to suspect something was wrong) when anything was out of the ordinary. Fear and superstition—old beliefs in magic things—played a huge role in the trials. People believed in witches and thought they could cause real harm through their powers.

The way the courts worked in the trials was also very unfair. Accused witches were brought before judges who already thought the accused people were evil witches. The accused then had to prove that they weren't witches. It's hard to argue against someone who already does not believe you. Also, the use of spectral evidence – the made-up ideas of the girls – made it almost impossible for people to defend themselves. It's even harder to argue against something totally made up! The community's fear and the judges' willingness to accept weak evidence led to tragic injustice.

There was a feeling all over town of fear and suspicion. Some people may have rushed to accuse others first, just to avoid being accused themselves. You might want to do that to your sibling at home when your parents catch you eating candy, but this was much, much more serious.

The Salem Witch Trials still fascinate people. They taught early Americans about the need for fair courts and the dangers of acting on superstition. The lasting memory—the legacy—of the events still reminds us today not to get caught up in fear.

As for Ann Putnam, her later apology is a powerful reminder of the importance of seeking forgiveness. Admitting you were wrong can be really hard, but it's a big step toward healing and moving on. So historical accounts remember Ann as a key accuser and also a figure of regret. Her story shows both that it can be dangerous to go along with the crowd and that it's never too late to say you're sorry.

DISCUSSION GUIDE

Review Questions:

1. How did Ann Putnam contribute to the Salem witch trials?

2. What type of evidence was often used in the trials, and why was it unreliable?

3. How did Ann Putnam seek forgiveness for her actions?

Discussion Questions:

1. Do you think fear can make people believe things or say things that aren't true? Can you think of a time when fear or rumors caused problems in history or in your own life?

2. Why is it important to stand up for what is right, even if it is difficult?

3. How do you think the people of Salem felt about the trials afterward? How can admitting wrongdoing and seeking forgiveness help heal a community?

Project Idea:

Create a play or skit about Ann Putnam's testimony and apology. Include scenes where Ann accuses others of witchcraft and later seeks forgiveness. Think about the characters involved and how they were feeling.

In the trial, think about how Ann is caught up in the fear of the town, how she might have felt regret already. Think about how scared and angry the accused would be, how shocked and confused the audience might be.

When Ann seeks forgiveness think about the fear she felt and the shame of her past. Think about how those at her church might still be angry. Show how Ann and her audience have changed over the two scenes.

PART II

☆ ☆ ☆

YOUNG HEROES OF
THE AMERICAN REVOLUTION

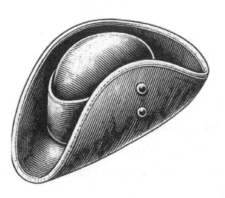

CHAPTER 3

JOSEPH PLUMB MARTIN (1760-1850)

WRITER OF THE REVOLUTION

I *magine being a young teenager and choosing to leave your home, your parents, and your friends to become a soldier in a war. When Joseph Plumb Martin was only fifteen years old, he did just that. He left his home in Connecticut and joined the Continental Army. It was June 1776, and the fight for American independence was in full swing. Little did Joseph know then that his experiences would one day provide perhaps the best report of what it was like to be a common soldier during the Revolution. Here is Joseph's fascinating story.*

Joseph's family had a history of military service, and he joined the Army because he wanted to be part of that. At fifteen, Joseph was younger than most other soldiers, but he was determined to do his share. His early days in the Army were hard for him. He had to learn to take orders, handle a gun, set up camp and carry supplies, and his days were filled with tough work and pain. Joseph quickly realized that being a soldier was not just about fighting – there was a lot of waiting, marching, and dealing with harsh living conditions.

He also took part in several key battles, including the Battle of Brooklyn in New York in 1776 and the Siege of Yorktown, Virginia in 1781, which won the Revolution for the Colonies. During these battles, he was still just a teenager, facing dangers and challenges that would be hard for any adult, let alone a young boy.

What really sets Joseph Plumb Martin apart is not only his youthful service but his role as a writer about the war. Many years after the war, Joseph wrote a book titled A Narrative of Some of the Adventures, Dangers and Sufferings of a Revolutionary Soldier. This book is a rare and valuable history of the Revolutionary War—told by someone who was actually there! Instead of just focusing on battles, Joseph wrote about the everyday lives of the soldiers who fought alongside him. He wanted people to remember what they went through.

From Joseph's book we found out that the soldiers often faced hunger, cold, and exhaustion. They often had few supplies and had to make do with what they had. They slept in tents or on the ground, with little protection from bad weather. He tells about the pain of long marches and the fear of the constant threat of enemy attacks. Despite these challenges, Joseph continued to believe in the goal of independence. So we learned from Joseph that the soldiers were really determined.

Joseph's book is particularly powerful because he wrote with such clear, plain detail, so you feel like you're there when you read it. He included specific tales that highlight the daily struggles of the soldiers. For example, Joseph wrote about a time when he and his friends had to eat "firecakes," which were flour and water mixed together and cooked on a rock. This might seem like a small thing, but it shows that the soldiers were pretty tough and clever.

His accounts of battle - his writings about fighting he saw - are just as specific. They paint a picture in your mind as you read. He wrote of a 1777 fight in Pennsylvania where they saw the British hiding behind a fence and charged at them, pushing them back through their campsite:

> "They left their kettles, in which they were cooking their breakfasts, on the fires, and some of their garments were lying on the ground, which the owners had not time to put on."

Joseph's memoirs have huge historical value. They provide a unique and personal view of the Revolutionary War. We wouldn't know about any of it if this teenager hadn't fearlessly joined the Army and been smart enough to remember so much. Joseph's life reminds us that American independence wasn't just won by famous generals—it was won by everyday soldiers who fought hard and never gave up, including one brave kid from Connecticut.

DISCUSSION GUIDE

Review Questions:

1. How old was Joseph Plumb Martin when he joined the Continental Army?

2. What were some of the hardships Joseph faced as a soldier?

3. Why are Joseph's memoirs important for understanding the Revolutionary War?

Discussion Questions:

1. Joseph wrote about how hard life was for soldiers, including times when they didn't have enough food or supplies. How do you think it felt to be a young soldier facing those challenges? What would you miss most if you were in his shoes? Do you think it would be harder on young soldiers or older soldiers?

2. Joseph had a ton to say about his time as a soldier. If you

could ask him one thing, what would it be?

3. Why do you think personal stories, such as Joseph's, are important for understanding history?

Project Idea:

Write a diary entry as if you were a soldier in the Revolutionary War. Describe a day in your life, including the details around when you get up, what you eat, who you talk to, where you go and the challenges you face. Talk about how you're feeling and what it's like being part of the war.

CHAPTER 4

SYBIL LUDINGTON (1761-1839)

TEENAGE PAUL REVERE

O n a dark, wet night in April 1777, sixteen-year-old Sybil Ludington faced a challenge that would test her courage and strength. The British were planning an attack on Danbury, Connecticut. This town was important because it held supplies for the Continental Army. Sybil's father, Colonel Henry Ludington, was in charge of the local militia, the townspeople who promised to fight as soldiers. But these soldiers were scattered in homes across the countryside, and someone needed to alert them. That someone would be Sybil. As soon as her father received the urgent news, Sybil offered to ride and warn the militia. She mounted her horse, Star, and set off into the stormy night.

Sybil's route covered nearly forty miles, more than twice the distance of Paul Revere's famous ride. She rode through woods and across streams, facing the risk of seeing British soldiers, bandits or wild animals. The rain poured down, making the ride even more dangerous.

Sybil's mission was big. She had to go to all the soldiers' houses and get them to defend Danbury. Every minute counted. Was she scared? Of course. But her determination and bravery kept her going. She pounded on doors, shouting the alarm and urging the men to gather at her dad's farm. The sense of urgency was all around her. Sybil knew that if she failed, things would be terrible.

But thanks to her warnings, about 400 militiamen were able to gather quickly. They found a way to confront the British troops and slow them down. Though the British did manage to burn some supplies, Sybil's actions helped save many more. Her bravery ensured that the Continental Army kept enough equipment to keep fighting.

To understand Sybil Ludington's ride, we need to look at what was going on in the American Revolution in 1777. At that time, the war had been raging for two years. The Continental Army, led by George Washington, faced many challenges. They were often outnumbered and lacked supplies. The British had the advantage of a well-organized army. Still, the Americans had the advantage of fighting on their home turf. They used quick information to stay one step ahead of the British.

Communication in the 1700s was nothing like it is today. There were no phones or internet. Messages had to be delivered by hand, often over long distances. This made riders like Sybil incredibly important. They were the lifeline that connected different parts of the Army and made sure that everyone was working together. Think about it – to put up a good defense, you needed to know where the enemy was, how many there were and what kind of weapons they had. If you didn't send enough soldiers, you could be defeated, but if you sent too many, you might lose a battle somewhere else. So the ability to gather information and act on it quickly meant the difference between victory and defeat. To act fast, the Americans depended on local folks to talk to their friends and neighbors. Sybil's mission was a great example. And she was just a kid.

Though Sybil wasn't immediately famous like Paul Revere, her story has been remembered and celebrated over time. Her ride has become legendary, and a statue of her on horseback in Carmel, New York, is an awesome tribute. In many ways, Sybil has become a symbol of courage and patriotism. Some historians argue about the exact facts of her ride, but the spirit of her brave tale remains powerful. It also reminds us that it's important to seek the truth when you study the past. However, the bigger lessons we can learn may still be valuable even if some of the details are lost to history.

DISCUSSION GUIDE

Review Questions:

1. How old was Sybil at the time of her ride in April 1777?

2. What was the purpose of Sybil's ride? How far did she go?

3. Why was it dangerous?

Discussion Questions:

1. Why do you think Sybil Ludington's ride is an important story in American history?

2. How can kids show bravery in today's communities?

3. What would you do if you had an important message that needed to be delivered right away? How would you make sure people listened?

Project Idea:

Create a modern-day equivalent (similar) mission where you must move fast through your community to send a message, gather people, or escape.

Maybe there is an illness that is spreading or a fire. How much time do you have? How many people need to know?

Make a map and a path and goals for the mission. This can help you understand Sybil's challenges and the importance of her mission.

CHAPTER 5

PETER FRANCISCO (1760-1831)

THE BOY-GIANT OF THE REVOLUTION

H e was a super-strong, six-and-a-half-foot giant during a time when people were much smaller than they are today. He became a legend for his feats in battle during the American Revolution. He was known as a "one-man army"... But the truth is that he was not yet a man! He was just a 16-year-old when he became a soldier fighting for independence. You're going to want to read more about Peter Francisco.

Peter's story begins with a mystery. As a young boy, he was found abandoned on the docks of City Point, Virginia. No one knew where he came from or who his parents were. Some say he was kidnapped from his home in the Azores, a group of islands off the coast of Portugal, and brought to America. Whatever the truth, Peter was taken in by Judge Anthony Winston, who raised him as his own. Growing up in Virginia, Peter learned to farm and work with his hands. He quickly showed that he was not like other boys. He was big and strong, even as a child. By the time Peter was a teenager, he stood over six feet tall and had the strength to match his size. This guy was a hulk.

Peter's physical strength and bravery became legendary during the Revolutionary War. He joined the Continental Army in Virginia in 1776 and took part in many key battles. As a teenager, he fought at Brandywine (Pennsylvania) in 1777, Germantown (Pennsylvania) in 1777 and Monmouth (New Jersey) in 1778. In 1779, he helped General "Mad" Anthony Wayne take a British fort with a daring nighttime raid at Stony Point, New York.

One of the most famous stories about him is from the Battle of Camden in South Carolina in 1780. As the battle was ending, Peter picked up and carried a 350-pound cannon barrel off the battlefield. He wanted to make sure that the enemy did not steal the cannon. This incredible feat earned him the nickname "The Virginia Giant."

Peter was able to turn the tide of battles on his own. For instance, at the Battle of Guilford Courthouse in North Carolina in 1781, armed with only a sword, he is said to have killed eleven enemy soldiers all by himself. His courage and skill in battle inspired those around him and terrified his enemies.

The impact of Peter Francisco on the Revolutionary War was profound. At times when the Continental Army was struggling, heroes like Peter provided hope. Other soldiers looked up to him. They shared the legends of the Virginia Giant around the campfire. Even George Washington is said to have praised him, saying that Peter was crucial in winning key battles and, ultimately, the war.

Peter Francisco's legacy (his lasting fame) lives on today. He is remembered as one of the most remarkable figures of the Revolution. In New Bedford, Massachusetts, a monument celebrates his contributions to American history. It shows the pride of the many Portuguese Americans who live there now. The "Virginia Giant" continues to amaze students of Revolutionary War battles. In 1975, the U.S. Postal Service created a stamp honoring Peter.

Peter's strength and bravery in the Continental Army inspired the soldiers around him and all over the Colonies. He proved that no matter where someone comes from or how tough their start is, they can still make a difference and even make history.

Discussion Guide

Review Questions:

1. Where was Peter Francisco born?

2. Why was he called the "Virginia Giant"?

3. Can you name two battles he fought in?

Discussion Questions:

1. Peter was taken from his home as a child and had to make a life for himself. How do you think his early struggles helped shape him into the hero he became?

2. Why do you think Peter Francisco is remembered today?

3. What does "strength" mean to you? Do you have to be huge to have "strength"? What other kinds of "strength" are there?

4. Can you think of anyone who is famous today for being strong? Who are the strong people in your life?

Project Idea:

Have a race where you add the challenge of carrying something kind of heavy – *safely*! See who can take it the farthest or the fastest. This can help you understand how strong Peter Francisco must have been to carry that cannon barrel.

CHAPTER 6

PHILLIS WHEATLEY (1753-1784)

THE YOUNG POET

C ould you write a poem that was so good that it changed history? That's what Phillis Wheatley did. Phillis, a young African American girl, wrote six verses praising George Washington. When he read her words, they changed him. Her powerful poetry showed him the potential and talent of African Americans. This was not just a simple poem. It was historic.

Phillis Wheatley's story begins thousands of miles away from America. She was born around 1753 in present-day Senegal, West Africa. When she was seven years old, she was captured by slave traders and brought to Boston on a boat named Phillis. She was given the name of the ship. The Wheatley family bought Philis at a slave auction. They saw something special in her and decided to educate her. This was unusual, as most enslaved people were not given the chance to learn. The Wheatleys taught Phillis to read and write in English. She quickly showed a talent for languages, and she then also learned Latin and Greek.

As she grew, Phillis's talent for writing poetry blossomed. She wrote her first poem at a young age and continued to write verses that amazed those who read them. Her first published poem, "On Messrs. Hussey and Coffin," came out in 1767. She was only fourteen years old, but her poems were filled with powerful ideas about freedom, faith, and doing what's right. Through her writing, Phillis shared her thoughts and feelings about the world around her in a way that was wise beyond her years.

As she grew, Phillis's talent for writing poetry blossomed. She wrote her first poem at a young age and continued to write verses that amazed those who read them. Her first published poem, "On Messrs. Hussey and Coffin," came out in 1767. She was only fourteen years old, but her poems were filled with powerful ideas about freedom, faith, and doing what's right. Through her writing, Phillis shared her thoughts and feelings about the world around her in a way that was wise beyond her years.

In 1773, Phillis published a book titled *Poems on Various Subjects, Religious and Moral*. This was a big accomplishment, especially for a young African American woman in the 18th century. Her book gained attention in America and even in Europe. Her poetry opened doors that had long been closed to people of African descent. By sharing her voice through her poems, Phillis helped challenge the views of her time and inspired other African Americans to write and speak out.

Phillis wrote the poem about George Washington when he was a general leading the American troops in the Revolution in 1776. She wrote:

> Proceed, great chief, with virtue on thy side,
> Thy ev'ry action let the Goddess guide.
> A crown, a mansion, and a throne that shine,
> With gold unfading, Washington! Be thine.

This poem means that she wanted Washington to win the war and that he was doing the right thing. She wanted him to have a golden crown and throne. He read the poem and liked it so much that he wrote her a letter and asked to see her if she were in Cambridge. It is said that Washington was so impressed by Phillis that he decided that other African Americans should be part of the Revolution and join the Army. Having African Americans in the fight changed the way other Americans saw them, and it shifted views on slavery. All that because of Phillis's poem! Her words were a spark that ignited a fire for equality.

Phillis Wheatley's work continues to inspire people to this day. She is remembered as a pioneer in African American literature and a symbol of the power of education. Philis also reminds us that you don't need super-strength to make a difference, that the pen is often mightier than the sword.

DISCUSSION GUIDE

Review Questions:

1. How old was Phillis Wheatley when she was captured and brought to America?

2. What languages did Phillis learn besides English?

3. What was the title of Phillis's first published book of poems?

Discussion Questions:

1. How did education help Phillis Wheatley overcome some of the challenges she faced?

2. Why do you think Phillis Wheatley's poetry was so powerful and influential? Why do you think words can be powerful even when someone doesn't have much power in their life?

3. Phillis used poetry to express her ideas and feelings. What's a way that you like to express yourself—through writing, drawing, music, or something else?

Project Idea:

Write a poem inspired by Phillis Wheatley's style. Think about themes that are important to you, such as freedom, hope, or justice. Use simple but powerful words to express your thoughts and feelings. Share the poem, and explain why it means something to you.

PART III

☆ ☆ ☆

TRAILBLAZERS OF THE EARLY REPUBLIC

CHAPTER 7

SACAGAWEA (1788-1812)

TEENAGE NATIVE GUIDE

A round 1800, a native village was brutally attacked by another tribe, and a young girl was captured and taken away. But she survived. She learned to live in her new surroundings. She went from being a lost captive to becoming an essential guide for one of the most famous expeditions in American history. That is the actual story of Sacagawea. How did that happen? Let's read about how this teenage girl was simply remarkable.

Born around 1788 near what is now the Idaho-Montana border, Sacagawea belonged to the Shoshone tribe of Native Americans. She lived a peaceful life with her family until one tragic day when she was about twelve years old. A Hidatsa tribe raiding party attacked her village, capturing her and many others. They took her to their villages to the east, where they enslaved her. Life with the Hidatsa was difficult, but Sacagawea adapted. She learned their language and customs. And you may have already guessed that knowing many languages and tribes would later prove very valuable...

But first, Sacagawea's life took another big turn when she was taken by Toussaint Charbonneau, a French-Canadian fur trader, and she became one of his wives around 1804. At this time, Meriwether Lewis and William Clark were planning their expedition to explore America's new Louisiana Territory. President Thomas Jefferson asked Lewis and Clark to map the land, study its resources, and set up relationships with the Native American tribes. The Lewis and Clark Expedition, which was also called the Corps of Discovery, needed someone who could help guide them through the vast, unmapped territory. Sacagawea, with her unique skills, was the right choice for the team.

When Sacagawea met Lewis and Clark, she was pregnant with a baby boy. But she still joined the expedition as an interpreter and guide. Her language abilities were critical. She spoke Shoshone, Hidatsa, and some French, which helped the team communicate with various tribes. Her knowledge of the land was equally important. Sacagawea knew the terrain and could locate food and water in the wild. She helped find edible plants, made moccasins and clothing, and cared for her newborn son, Jean Baptiste, after he was born on the journey.

Sacagawea was also a smart leader. When the expedition's boat nearly capsized (flipped over into the water), Sacagawea quickly saved journals and maps, keeping the most valuable information from being washed away. Her calm and fast thinking impressed the entire team. She was only 17 years old.

Sacagawea made many contributions to the overall success of the expedition. One of her most important moments came when the Corps of Discovery encountered the Shoshone tribe. The team needed horses to cross the Rocky Mountains, and Sacagawea recognized the Shoshone chief as her brother, Cameahwait. This reunion was emotional and vital. It helped everyone get along, and Lewis and Clark got the much-needed horses and also a Shoshone guide. Sacagawea made sure the interactions between the expedition and the Native Americans were peaceful.

To understand the significance of Sacagawea's role, it helps to know more about the Lewis and Clark Expedition. The Louisiana Purchase in 1803 was a huge event. President Thomas Jefferson negotiated the purchase of land from France, doubling the size of the United States. This new territory needed to be explored and mapped. Jefferson wanted to set up an American hold on the land before European powers could claim it. He also hoped to find a water route to the Pacific Ocean. This first American exploration of the Louisiana Purchase was crucial for

American expansion and development. It opened up new opportunities for trade, settlement, and scientific discovery.

The Lewis and Clark Expedition's journey was filled with challenges and discoveries. They traveled thousands of miles from the Dakotas to the Pacific Northwest in harsh weather, over rough land, risking fights with Native Americans. Sacagawea helped the team find safe paths, locate resources, and establish friendly relations with local tribes. Americans saw the mission as successful. It provided important facts about the new territory's geography, plants, animals, and people. It also paved the way for further exploration and settlement. And it never would have happened that way without a teenager named Sacagawea.

DISCUSSION GUIDE

Review Questions:

1. What tribe did Sacagawea belong to before she was captured?

2. What languages did she speak?

3. What did she save when the expedition's boat nearly capsized?

Discussion Questions:

1. Why do you think Lewis and Clark believed Sacagawea was the right person to help with the expedition?

2. How did Sacagawea's skills and knowledge help the expedi-

tion succeed? What would they have done without her?

3. Sacagawea helped guide Lewis and Clark across lands they didn't know. If you could take an adventure to explore a new place, where would you go and why?

Project Idea:

Create a map of Sacagawea's life and journey with the Lewis and Clark Expedition. Show significant points along the expedition's route including timing of each stop. This will help you understand the incredible distance she traveled and the different landscapes she knew. Research the expedition's route, or start with a list of some key locations and dates below:

- Corps Starts at St. Louis, Missouri (May 14, 1804)

- Sacagawea's Birthplace – near present-day Salmon, Idaho (Born around 1788)

- Fort Mandan (She joins Corps) – near Washburn, North Dakota (Winter 1804-1805, joined in Nov. 1804, baby born Feb. 1805)

- The Missouri River Route – through Present-Day North and South Dakota, Nebraska, Iowa, and Kansas (Apr.-June 1805)

- Rocky Mountains Crossing – Lemhi Pass (Montana-Idaho Border) (Aug. 1805, meets with brother, gets horses)

- End of the Journey (Pacific Ocean) – Near Astoria, Oregon (Dec. 1805-Mar. 1806, winter camp before going home)

CHAPTER 8

DAVID FARRAGUT (1801-1870)

YOUNG NAVY LEADER

During the War of 1812 between the Americans and the British, a 12-year-old boy was put in charge of an entire warship thousands of miles from home. You see, young David Farragut had already shown that he could stay calm and be brave during battle. So when his American ship captured a British ship called the Barclay in the Pacific Ocean, the captain put David in charge of the newly taken Barclay.

For weeks, David commanded the sailors on the Barclay all on his own, and he wasn't even a teenager. In time, David would go on to lead whole fleets. But this was where it all began — on a small, captured British ship, across the world, where a boy proved that he was a commander in the making.

David Farragut's early life was far from ordinary. Born in 1801, he faced hardship early on. His mother died when he was just seven years old. His father had David live with Navy Captain David Porter in Virginia. As a foster child, David learned the ropes of sea life from a young age.

Captain Porter became a father to him, and David even changed his name from James to David in honor of his foster father.

David Farragut's naval career began at the tender age of nine. Imagine being on a warship at nine! David joined the Navy in 1810, and his first real test came during the War of 1812. David was assigned to the ship, the *Essex*. The *Essex* was part of the U.S. Navy's plan to stop British ships from trading in the Pacific. The *Essex* raided British vessels, stole their cargo and even captured some boats. That is how David ended up commanding the *Barclay*.

Eventually, the *Essex* lost a bloody battle to two British ships, and David was taken as a prisoner of war. But aboard the *Essex* and the *Barclay*, David gained incredible experience. He was part of chases on the high seas and dangerous battles. He had taken command of a ship of his own. He had even been a prisoner. But most importantly, he had shown that he was a leader and that he could make smart, quick decisions at a young age. He stood out as a sailor with a bright future.

The War of 1812 was a big moment in David's career, but this war often doesn't get talked about much in history books. This war between America and Britain lasted from 1812 to 1815. One of the leading causes was that Britain was blocking American ships from trading with France because Britain was at war with France. Another major cause was something called *impressment*, where British ships captured American sailors and forced them to serve in the British Navy.

Some of the main events of the War of 1812 included the British burning of America's capital, Washington, D.C., in 1814, and the battle for Fort McHenry in Baltimore, where Frances Scott Key wrote the American national anthem, the Star-Spangled Banner. One of the last major battles was the Battle of New Orleans, where General Andrew Jackson led American forces to victory. However, because communication was much slower then, the battle actually took place after the war ended! The war ended with the Treaty of Ghent in 1814. No land changed hands due to the conflict, but the War of 1812 helped the new U.S. prove it could stand up to a world power and pushed the growth of American military and territory.

After the War of 1812, David Farragut continued to serve in the U.S. Navy. His brave tactics changed naval warfare. One of his most famous moments came during the Civil War at the Battle of Mobile Bay, Alabama. Fighting for the Union, David's ship was sailing through dangerous waters filled with exploding traps, then called "torpedoes." Some leaders might have turned back, but Farragut gave his famous command, "Damn the torpedoes!.. Full speed ahead!" His bold decision led to a huge Union victory.

Farragut did more than show bravery in battle. He was a giant in the growth of the U.S. Navy. His career was more than 50 years long, and he helped the Navy go from a small fleet of wooden sailing ships to a large fleet of iron steam-powered vessels. He became the first full Admiral in U.S. naval history in 1866. Today, in Washington, D.C., Farragut Square, a statue and two subway stations are all named for him. He is remembered a tough, smart, patriotic sailor, and it all started when he was just a boy.

DISCUSSION GUIDE

Review Questions:

1. How old was David Farragut when he first joined the Navy?

2. What famous command did Farragut give during the Battle of Mobile Bay?

3. What was the significance of the War of 1812 for the United States?

Discussion Questions:

1. David changed his name to match his foster father's. Are you named after anyone? Do you know someone who is? What other big things do people do to show someone their

thankfulness and love?

2. Why is strong leadership important in difficult situations? Do you think kids today are ready to be leaders like David was at age 12?

3. Have you ever volunteered for something you weren't sure you could do? How did it turn out?

Project Idea:

Build small models of the USS Essex, a ship from the War of 1812 called a "frigate."

For the hull, use materials such as popsicle sticks or plastic straws glued together or shape a sponge or block of Styrofoam.

Use plastic straws or pencils for masts and paper or foam sheets for the sails.

See which ship floats the best and moves fastest. This activity helps you understand the challenges of shipbuilding and the importance of naval innovation.

CHAPTER 9

KIT CARSON (1809-1868)

THE SCOUT BOY OF THE WILD WEST

W hen he was only 16, Kit Carson decided to set out on his own. In 1826, he left his mother, his home, and his job training to be a saddlemaker in Missouri. Young Kit boldly joined a train of wagons heading to Santa Fe, then part of Mexico. Before he even turned 20, Kit had become a skilled fur trapper living in the wilderness. He would go on to be one of the most famous scouts in American history.

Kit Carson was born in Kentucky in December 1809. His early life was a mix of adventure and hardship. When he was just two years old, his family moved to Missouri. This was the frontier, where life was rough and full of challenges. Because of fighting with Native Americans, the Carsons had to build a fort of high fenceposts around their home and stand guard with guns while they worked on their farmland. Kit's father died in a farming accident when Kit was only eight, leaving a wife and 15 children. Kit had to learn how to hunt for food and find his way through the forests and plains. By the time he was a teenager, Kit already knew how to survive in the wild.

Kit was soon on his own in Santa Fe. He found work as a cook, but he wanted more adventure. He left Santa Fe and used his cooking and camping skills to become a trapper. Trapping meant catching animals for their fur, or pelts, mostly from beavers, which lots of folks wanted to buy around the U.S. and even in Europe for hats and other clothes. People soon paid Kit to help them trap and to keep them from getting lost. He also helped keep travelers fed and safe and ensured they got along with the Native Americans they met.

The fur trade was a big part of life on the frontier and a reason people went west. Trapping could pay lots of money, but it was dangerous. Trappers would spend months in the wilderness without the safety, food and shelter of towns. People like Kit were very valuable – everyone likes to go camping, but maybe not for months and months!

With the knowledge he got as a boy, Kit later became a famous scout and explorer as an adult. One of his most notable roles was as a scout for John C. Frémont's expeditions in the 1840s. Frémont, an explorer and U.S. military officer, hired Kit to guide his team through the challenges of the Rocky Mountains. They helped map the American West and the trails, allowing settlers to move to Oregon and California.

During the Mexican-American War, Kit Carson's skills were really put to the test. He served as a scout and delivered important messages to get troops through enemy territory. Kit helped America claim California. Fremont sent reports back east telling how brave Kit was, and when people read the reports around the country, Kit became famous. He made people proud and excited about a hero with special skills in the Wild West.

Today, Kit is remembered as a symbol of the toughness of frontier Americans. The capital of Nevada, Carson City, is named for him, and his home in Taos, New Mexico, is a museum. But it was what he learned as a boy and the adventures he faced as a teenager that made him so good at what he did.

DISCUSSION GUIDE

Review Questions:

    1. How old was Kit Carson when he set out on his own?

2. Who hired Kit Carson to guide his expeditions through the Rocky Mountains?

3. What role did Kit Carson play in the Mexican-American War?

Discussion Questions:

1. What qualities make a good scout?

2. How do you think Kit Carson's early experiences helped him later in life?

3. Kit traveled all over the country even before he grew up. Where would you like to go most in America?

Project Idea:

Design a survival guide based on Kit Carson's experiences. Create sections and include illustrations showing what to eat, where to sleep, how to travel, and how to get supplies. This will help you understand the skills needed to survive in the wild and appreciate the expertise of frontiersmen like Kit Carson.

CHAPTER 10

OLIVE OATMAN (1837-1903)

THE CAPTIVE WHO BRIDGED TWO WORLDS

*P*icture this: you're 14 years old and moving from Illinois to California, dreaming of a better life, better weather and a fresh start. For Olive Oatman, that dream turned into a nightmare. In 1851, on her way west, Olive's family was attacked; her parents were killed, and she and her little sister were taken prisoner. But that's just the beginning of Olive's incredible story. Let's keep learning.

Olive Oatman was born in 1837 in rural Illinois. Seeking new opportunities, her family joined a wagon train bound for California in 1851. This wasn't just any road trip. It was dangerous, with mountains to pass and possible attacks by Native Americans. As the wagons traveled through present-day Arizona, tragedy struck. The family was ambushed by the Yavapai tribe. Olive and her younger sister, Mary Ann, were kidnapped. The rest of their family was killed. Imagine the terror and confusion Olive felt. She was thrust into a new life at 14. All new faces, new languages and new surroundings with the Yavapai.

Things got better when Olive and Mary Ann were traded from the Yavapai to the Mohave tribe about a year later. At first, Olive didn't know what to expect, but she quickly realized that the Mohave treated her and her sister kindly. They gave the girls food, clothes, and shelter. Olive even learned their language and customs. One of the most significant moments in Olive's time with the Mohave was when they tattooed her chin and arms, a sign that she was being accepted into their tribe. Take a look at the pictures of Olive in this book.

Life was still hard, though. Sadly, Mary Ann didn't survive due to food shortages. This was a heartbreaking time for Olive, but she stayed strong and continued to live among the Mohave for several more years. By the time she was 19, she had fully adapted to her new life and was seen as part of the community.

In 1856, Olive's life changed once again. American soldiers found out about her and got the Mohave to release her. The Mohave were sad to see her go. Olive returned to American society, where her story fascinated everyone. Coming back to life among settlers wasn't always easy for Olive. She had been through a lot, and her tattoos permanently marked her as different. But when life gave her lemons, she made lemonade. She wrote a book about her experiences and traveled to share her story. She taught a powerful lesson in tolerance of other cultures and acceptance of differences.

Settlers had difficult and sometimes dangerous lives when they moved West. While settlers faced risks, their push for more land had an even greater impact on Native communities over time. Olive's story is an important reminder of these struggles. She experienced both sides of life on the frontier and became a human bridge between two cultures. Before turning 20, she was already a symbol of the American frontier.

DISCUSSION GUIDE

Review Questions:

1. How old was Olive Oatman when she was captured by the Yavapai tribe?

2. What marked Olive's inclusion into the Mohave tribe?

3. What did Olive do after her return to American society?

Discussion Questions:

1. Do you know anyone who is growing up in a very different culture from a parent's childhood culture?

2. Olive's life changed when she was taken captive. How do you think she had to adapt to survive?

3. After returning to her old life, Olive shared what she learned from the Mojave people. Why do you think it's important to learn from different cultures and experiences?

Project Ideas:

1. **Create a diary entry from Olive Oatman's perspective.** Imagine what her daily life was like with the Mohave tribe and how she felt during her rescue and return to American society. This will help you understand her experiences and the challenges she faced.

2. **Act out a news interview with Olive.** Have one person act as Olive just after she has returned to American society. Have everyone else ask questions, such as: *what was the hardest part of your journey? How did you feel when you lived with the Mohave? What do you want people to understand about your experience?* Have thoughtful questions and answers. This will help you understand what it must have been like for Olive to live among the Native Americans and to come back. As a bonus, record or perform the interview for an audience.

PART IV

☆ ☆ ☆

COURAGEOUS KIDS OF THE CIVIL WAR

CHAPTER 11

JOHNNY CLEM (1851-1937)

THE DRUMMER BOY OF CHICKAMAUGA

J ohnny Clem wasn't your average kid — he was a boy with a serious plan. When the Civil War began, Johnny was only nine years old, but he wanted badly to join the Army and make a difference. Despite being turned away because of his age, Johnny refused to give up. He ran away from home and followed the soldiers. By the time he was 12, Johnny had fought and proven his courage on the battlefield and become famous by a nickname, the "Drummer Boy of Chickamauga." How did a boy become a hero? Let's find out.

Johnny Clem was born on August 13, 1851, in Newark, Ohio. As a young boy, he was interested in the military and being a soldier. Johnny was nine years old when the Civil War began in 1861. When he tried to join the Union Army, they said no and that he was too young. But Johnny went with the soldiers anyway, following them on their marches from camp to camp, battle to battle. He carried a drum almost as big as he was!

Johnny stuck around and became the mascot and unofficial drummer boy for the 22nd Michigan Infantry. The soldiers took a liking to him, and the officers even paid his salary out of their own pockets. Johnny's determination finally paid off when he was officially allowed to enlist in 1863.

Being a drummer boy was an important role. Drummer boys had to keep the beat during marches and signal orders during battles. The powerful sound of drums helped soldiers get over their fears. Johnny quickly adapted to his new duties. He was eager to prove himself, and he worked hard. Despite his young age, Johnny became known for his cheerful spirit and willingness to face danger right along with the men.

The Battle of Chickamauga in Georgia was when things really changed for Johnny. Fought in September 1863, it was one of the major battles of the Civil War, involving large numbers of troops on both sides. Johnny, now twelve years old, found himself in the thick of the fighting. During the battle, he got lost from his side and found himself face-to-face with a Confederate officer. The officer ordered Johnny to surrender, but Johnny had other ideas. He fired his musket, hitting the officer and saving his own life. No one could believe that a boy had acted so tough in the face of danger. This act of bravery earned him the nickname "The Drummer Boy of Chickamauga" and made him a national hero.

The Civil War began in 1861 and lasted until 1865. It was fought between the Northern states (the Union) and the Southern states (the Confederacy) when the South tried to leave the U.S. to maintain slavery. The disagreement over slavery had been growing for many years. What resulted was the deadliest war in American history, and in the end the South surrendered; the country stayed one nation, and slavery was abolished.

For people in Johnny Clem's hometown in Ohio, the Civil War meant constant worry and fear. Families sent their loved ones to fight, never knowing if they would return. The war affected everyone, from farmers to shopkeepers. It disrupted daily life in countless ways as lots of men left and didn't come back. The Battle of Chickamauga, where Johnny earned his fame, was one of the war's bloodiest battles. The bravery shown by soldiers like Johnny played a crucial role in the Union's eventual victory.

Johnny Clem had a long successful military career started by his heroics at Chickamauga. After the battle, he was promoted to sergeant, making him the youngest to hold that rank in the U.S. Army. That set the stage for a proud life in the Army. Johnny rose through the ranks and finally retired as a major general, having dedicated years to serving his country. Johnny's story is a reminder of the courage and determination of young soldiers who fought in the Civil War.

DISCUSSION GUIDE

Review Questions:

1. How old was Johnny Clem when he first tried to join the Union Army?

2. What was Johnny Clem's role in the Army before he officially enlisted?

3. Why did Johnny Clem become famous at the Battle of Chickamauga?

Discussion Questions:

1. What qualities do you think made Johnny Clem a good soldier despite his young age?

2. How can young people show bravery in their own lives today? Think about times you are afraid and how you overcome it.

3. Drummer boys helped keep soldiers brave. What kind of music or sounds do you use to get pumped-up and confident?

Project Idea:

Create a drum using household items. For the drum, find an empty soup can, coffee tin or oatmeal container. Cut the neck off of a balloon and stretch the rest of the balloon over the top of the can [note: you can also use packing tape instead of a balloon]. Wrap a rubber band or packing tape around the can to keep the balloon in place. For drumsticks, use unsharpened pencils or wooden spoon handles. Decorate the side of the drum with symbols of the Army – an eagle, a star or a flag. Now, play a tune that you think would help soldiers remain brave. Try marching and playing together. This activity will help you appreciate the role of drummer boys like Johnny Clem and understand the rhythms that guided soldiers during the Civil War.

CHAPTER 12

THE SONS OF FREDERICK DOUGLASS: LEWIS (1840-1908), FREDERICK JR. (1842-1892), CHARLES (1844-1920)

A FAMILY OF ABOLITIONISTS

Meet Lewis, Frederick Jr., and Charles Douglass, the sons of the legendary abolitionist Frederick Douglass. They got to grow up with a dad who was a hero to many, constantly speaking out against slavery and fighting for freedom. But the Douglass brothers weren't just sitting around listening to their dad — they had their own adventures, even serving as soldiers in the Civil War. In fact, while they were still boys, the brothers helped their father fight for freedom. Want to know what these brave young men did? Let's read on.

Before the Civil War, the Douglass brothers were already making their mark where they lived in Rochester, New York. All three boys helped their father with his newspaper, The North Star, which he published to spread his abolitionist message. Abolitionists were people who believed in abolishing - getting rid of - slavery. Lewis, the oldest Douglass brother, learned the skills of typesetting and printing, and his younger brothers, Frederick Jr. and Charles, soon did the same.

The brothers also supported their father's work on the Underground Railroad. The Underground Railroad was not an actual train but a network of people and homes that helped slaves escape to the North. This was dangerous work; they risked their lives to help others, often hiding escaped slaves who were being chased and assisting them on their journey to safety. By the time they were teenagers, Lewis, Frederick Jr., and Charles were actively participating in their father's mission, showing the same courage and determination to fight against injustice.

Lewis Douglass, the oldest, was born in 1840, so he was 21 when the Civil War broke out in 1861. Inspired by his father's fight for freedom, he joined the 54th Massachusetts Infantry Regiment in 1863, one of the first African American units in the Union Army. At 23, Lewis then served as a sergeant and quickly became known for his courage. He fought in the Battle of Fort Wagner, one of the most dangerous battles African American soldiers faced. Lewis showed tremendous bravery as he led his men through heavy gunfire. Although Lewis was wounded, he survived and continued his service, writing letters about his experiences. Even at a young age, Lewis was a leader, just like his father.

Frederick Douglass Jr., born in 1842, was two years younger than Lewis. When the Civil War began, he was just 19 years old. Motivated by his father's abolitionist cause, Frederick Jr. helped recruit African American soldiers for the Union Army even before he joined himself. He later enlisted in the 5th Massachusetts Cavalry, an African American regiment. As a teenager, Frederick Jr. had already proven his bravery by helping his father in dangerous situations on the Underground Railroad. In the war, his experiences helped him inspire others to face danger in the fight for freedom.

Charles Douglass, the youngest brother, was born in 1844, making him four years younger than Lewis and two years younger than Frederick Jr. When the war started, he was just 17 years old. Even though he was the youngest, Charles was eager to follow in his older brothers' footsteps. He joined the 54th Massachusetts Infantry Regiment in 1863, the same unit as his brother, Lewis. Although Charles faced illness and was eventually released from the Army due to health reasons, his willingness to serve demonstrated his commitment to his family's legacy in the battle for abolition.

Growing up, the Douglass brothers had a front-row seat to history. Their father's work as an abolitionist meant they often faced danger and were constantly on the move. But it also meant that they learned from his bravery and determination to end slavery. Before any of them reached 20, they had not only helped with their father's newspaper, The North Star, and the Underground Railroad but also became soldiers in the Union Army, fighting for freedom. The Douglass brothers proved that courage runs in the family, standing up for what they believed in and helping to make history. How does your family pass down beliefs and traditions?

DISCUSSION GUIDE

Review Questions:

    1. What was the name of the Douglass newspaper?

    2. What was the Underground Railroad?

    3. How many of the Douglass sons joined the Union Army?

Discussion Questions:

    1. How do you think growing up in a household dedicated to abolition influenced Lewis, Charles, and Frederick Douglass Jr.?

    2. Why is it important for families to talk about issues such as

a conflict like the Civil War?

3. The Douglass family believed education was one of the most powerful tools for freedom. What's something you've learned in school that made you feel stronger or more confident?

Project Idea:

Plan a day where you go to work with a parent or spend the day learning about what a parent does. Take the time to understand what he or she does on a usual day. This activity can help you understand the importance of their work and how it contributes to your family and the community.

CHAPTER 13

EMMA EDMONDS (1841-1898)

THE SECRET SOLDIER

A young Union soldier crouched behind a tree, her breath slow and steady as a group of Confederate troops marched by. If they discovered her, she'd be in terrible danger. Her heart pounded, but she kept herself calm - she had lots of practice staying calm while staying secret. Not just because she was a good soldier but also because she was a woman pretending to be a man so she could stay in the Army.

This is the remarkable story of Emma Edmonds, a woman who disguised herself as a man to fight in the Civil War. Some say she even became a spy, sneaking into enemy territory in disguise. But while we know for sure that she served as a soldier and nurse, there's no solid proof that she was ever actually a spy. Some historians think she may have made up parts of her story, while others believe her secret missions were real but never recorded. No matter what, one thing is clear—Emma's courage was real.

Emma was born in 1841 on a farm in Canada, where her life was tough. Her father was strict and believed girls should stick to cooking and sewing. But Emma had other dreams. She wanted adventure, freedom, and a life beyond the farm. So, as a teenager, she made a bold choice—she cut her hair, dressed as a man, and ran away to America. From that moment on, she was no longer Emma Edmonds. She was Franklin Thompson, a traveling Bible salesman.

When the Civil War started in 1861, Emma was just 19, but she felt a strong pull to help the Union cause. Women weren't allowed to fight, but as Franklin, she found a way. She signed on with the 2nd Michigan Infantry as a field nurse. It was dangerous, exhausting work. Emma had to be careful to never let anyone suspect her secret. She learned to move, speak, and act like the other soldiers. She slept in crowded tents, marched in the heat, and tended to wounded men on battlefields.

Years later, Emma wrote that she had done even more than nursing—she claimed she had also worked as a Union spy. In her stories, she disguised herself as different characters, including a Southern man named Charles Mayberry and an Irish peddler woman named Bridget O'Shea. She wrote that when she pretended to be Mayberry, she was able to make friends with Confederates and trick them into giving away the names of their secret agents. She said that while she was O'Shea, she pretended to sell soaps and fooled Confederates into telling her more about where they were going and where they were getting supplies.

However, historians cannot find government records to prove she was a spy. Some historians think she may have added exciting details to make her life sound more thrilling, while others believe she really did work in spying but that records were never kept. What we do know is that Emma had the skills to fool the people around her for years - the skills you'd need to be a good spy. So maybe her story is true?

In 1863, Emma's double life became too much. After two years of war, she became sick with malaria. She knew if she went to an army doctor, he would discover that Franklin Thompson was really Emma Edmonds. To protect her secret, she made a tough choice—she left the army camp to get better on her own. But because she left without permission, the Army labeled her a deserter, someone who leaves without permission.

Even though she had to leave, Emma didn't stop helping. Once she recovered, she continued to care for soldiers, working as a nurse for the rest of the war, this time as a woman, Emma. Many years later, her former fellow soldiers stood up for her. In 1884, the government erased her desertion charge, giving her an honorable discharge and a veteran's pension—a special payment for her past service. The Army recognized her as a hero.

Whether or not every part of her story is true, one thing is certain—Emma risked everything to serve her new country. Her life reminds us that much of history is full of mysteries, and often, no one still alive can tell us what actually happened. But Emma Edmonds was fearless. And that's a story worth telling.

DISCUSSION GUIDE

Review Questions:

1. Why did Emma leave Canada?

2. What was Emma Edmonds' male name when she joined the Union Army?

3. Name one of the disguises Emma said she used during her spy missions.

Discussion Questions:

1. Why do you think the Army paid her even though she broke the rules by joining as a woman?

2. Do you think Emma's stories of spying were true? How could her work be true but not have a record? If not true, why would she have told these stories?

3. Ema had to keep her identity a secret to serve in the Civil War. Have you ever had to keep a secret for a long time? Was it hard?

Project Idea:

Write a secret message in code as if you were Emma Edmonds. For example, try replacing each letter of a message with a symbol, number or different letter. Remember to use the same symbol each time you use that letter. And keep a key to the symbols you use so you can unlock the code and decode the message!

Have a friend try to decode the message without the key.

Think about how you would send important information without being discovered. This activity will help you understand the challenges and creativity required in espionage (another word for spying).

PART V

☆ ☆ ☆

YOUNG INVENTORS OF
THE INDUSTRIAL AGE

CHAPTER 14

George Westinghouse (1846-1914)

The Boy Who Loved Trains

P icture a little boy standing at a railroad station more than 150 years ago, his eyes wide with amazement as a massive steam engine rolls into the station and gradually comes to a stop, gasping and clanging. The loud whistles, the yelling of workers, and the sheer power of the train wow him. This boy is George Westinghouse, and his love for trains would lead him to change the world of railroads forever and save tons of lives.

Born on October 6, 1846, in Central Bridge, New York, George grew up during a time when steam engines and railroads meant progress and adventure. George's fascination with trains began early. His father owned a machine shop in Schenectady, where they made early machines for farmers, such as plows. They also made parts for steam engines and repaired machines that customers brought in. George spent countless hours at the shop watching his father work and tinkering with tools and machines. He was curious about how things worked and loved to take them apart and put them back together. This hands-on experience sparked his interest in engineering - the science of building and designing engines and machines.

By the time he was a teenager, George was already inventing his own gadgets and dreaming of ways to improve the world around him. When he was just 19, George invented a new rotary steam engine. This engine could make trains run with less fuel. This early accomplishment got him even more excited to create.

His next invention made a huge impact. Just three years later, George invented the air brake for trains. Before this invention, stopping a big, heavy, fast train was a slow and dangerous process. The brakemen had to run along the top of moving train cars to hit the brakes, risking their lives every time. George's air brake system used pumped air to apply the brakes on all the train cars at the same time. This made stopping much faster and much safer!

The air brake was a game-changer for the railroads. It greatly improved train travel as trains could stop more reliably – think about how much better it would be to ride on a train that stops when it is supposed to and no one gets injured. George founded the Westinghouse Air Brake Company to make and sell his invention. His air brake system became the top choice for trains across America and eventually around the world. George's invention saved riders, conductors and brakemen. His commitment to safety and innovation changed railroads forever.

George didn't stop there. He continued to invent. He created a way to measure the flow of water in pipes, which helped allow for city water systems. He also invented a device to get derailed train cars back on tracks, making it easier to deal with train accidents. George's inventions touched many parts of everyday life.

In the 1880s, George went into the new world of electricity. At that time, Thomas Edison was telling people to use direct current (DC) to send electric power from town to town. But George saw that alternating current (AC) was better because it could travel long distances without losing as much energy. One of the most significant moments for George's AC power system came at the World's Columbian Exposition in Chicago in 1893. George's company lit the fair, showing the power of AC electricity to millions of visitors. This event helped to make George's AC power the pick for electric power transmission. By 1896, George also used AC power to light the city of Buffalo, New York. Despite fierce opponents and safety concerns from DC fans, George's AC power system won. George's work in electricity changed how we use and send power today.

From a young boy fascinated by trains to a teenage inventor to a world-changer, George's life shows that curiosity, passion and hard work can lead to incredible accomplishments. To this day, when you hear an old train "hiss" after it stops, that's because of George's air brakes!

DISCUSSION GUIDE

Review Questions:

1. What did George's family do that helped him learn about machines?

2. Why were George's air brakes better for trains?

3. What was George's power system called?

Discussion Questions:

1. George was a curious kid, especially about trains and machines. What's something you're curious about right now, and how could you learn more about it?

2. How can improving safety help inspire inventions? Can you think of any inventions that made something safer?

3. Why do you think there was conflict between George and those who wanted DC power?

Project Idea:

Balloon Powered Brake Model: show how air pressure can stop motion, similar to George Westinghouse's air brake system.

Materials:

- A small toy car

- A balloon

- Rubber bands

- Plastic straw

- Tape

- Cardboard or a flat surface

Instructions:

- Attach the balloon to one end of the straw using a rubber band, ensuring it's airtight.

- Tape the straw securely to the toy car so the balloon inflates toward the rear of the car.

- Inflate the balloon and release it while holding the car still; then let it go [note: also try lightly pushing the car forward and watching how the air pushes it back].

- See how the air exiting the balloon pushes against the car, like a breaking force made with air.

CHAPTER 15

ALEXANDER GRAHAM BELL (1847-1922)

YOUNG EXPERIMENTER WITH SOUND

T hink about a world with no phones — no texting, no calling your friends, and no ordering pizza with a simple tap. Hard to picture, right? Well, Alexander Graham Bell is the man who helped change all of that. But before he invented the telephone, he was just a curious kid like you, fascinated by sound and how people communicate. Alexander's life was filled with amazing discoveries, and it all started when he was a kid.

Alexander was born on March 3, 1847, in Scotland. His family spent a lot of time studying sound and communication. Alexander's mother was deaf, and his father, an expert in speech, made a system to teach speech to people who were deaf. Imagine how hard it would be to learn speech if you couldn't hear. That was a daily focus of the Graham family.

Alexander's house was filled with books and gadgets related to his father's work, and Alexander was homeschooled by his dad. Alexander showed an interest in communications from an early age. By the time he was a teenager, he was already doing experiments with sound and vibrations. He was so fascinated by how sound works that he created his own invention to remove husks from wheat using noise vibrations!

Alexander even set up the machine in a barn at just 12 years old – he was an inventor as a boy!

But his real passion as a young man was helping deaf people like his mom. He wanted to help her communicate. He did all kinds of tests with sound, for example, using tuning forks and making tones with different materials to see how noise traveled. Alexander even created a device called a *harmonic telegraph* to send multiple messages over a single wire using different tones. This thinking showed how much he cared about connecting people.

This passion later led to his most famous invention, the telephone. Moving to the United States as a young man in 1871, Alexander tested ways to send sound over a distance. He was inspired by the telegraph, which allowed people to message with "dots" and "dashes" along wires, but he wanted to go a step further. He wanted to create a device that could carry the human voice. This idea drove him to work constantly, experimenting with all kinds of different designs.

The first successful telephone call took place on March 10, 1876, in Boston, Massachusetts. Alexander spoke the famous words to his assistant, "Mr. Watson, come here, I want to see you." Watson heard the voice clearly on the other end. What a moment! It proved that their device worked. This was a turning point. Those words and that invention would change the world in ways Alexander could hardly imagine.

The impact of the telephone was enormous. At first, people were unsure. They couldn't believe that voice could travel over wires. But as more people tried the phone, they saw its potential. Businesses quickly adopted the new technology. It allowed them to communicate instantly with customers and partners far away. The telephone network snowballed (grew quickly). By 1880, nearly 50,000 telephones were in use. This number continued to grow, making the world feel smaller and more connected.

The Industrial Revolution was a time of big changes, stretching from the late 1700s to the early 1900s. New inventions made life easier and faster. Factories took over, making products in large amounts instead of by hand. Steam engines powered trains and ships, making travel quicker. The telegraph let people send messages instantly over long distances. In the middle of all this innovation, Alexander's invention of the telephone was a perfect fit, changing the way people communicated forever.

Alexander actually didn't quit inventing after the telephone. He continued to come up with new ideas, including the metal detector and the audiometer, a device that tests hearing. Alexander Graham Bell's curiosity and drive to improve the world around him never stopped, but it all started with his boyhood experiments and inventions.

DISCUSSION GUIDE

Review Questions:

1. What was the first device Alexander Graham Bell invented as a child?

2. What were the first words spoken over the telephone?

3. How did Bell's work with the deaf community influence his inventions?

Discussion Questions:

1. How has the invention of the telephone changed how we communicate today as families, friends and businesses?

2. If you could invent a new way to talk to people across long distances, what would it be like?

3. How can inventions help people with special needs? Can you think of any other inventions that do that?

Project Idea:

Simple telephone using cups and string. You will need two plastic cups and a long piece of string.

Instructions:

- Punch a small hole in the bottom of each cup.

- Run each end of the string through a cup hole and tie knots inside the cups to keep the string from slipping out.

- Pull the cups apart so the string is tight. Have one person speak into one cup while the other listens through the second cup.

- See how far you can stretch the string and still hear each other. This project will help you understand the basic principles of how sound travels and the cleverness behind Bell's invention.

CHAPTER 16

FRANK EPPERSON (1894-1983)

FORTUNATE FREEZING

*D*o you ever like to experiment with different treats, like trying different candy toppings on ice cream or mixing different sprinkles on cookies? What if I told you that a kid was once experimenting just like you and invented one of the all-time favorite American treats – by accident? That's exactly what happened to eleven-year-old Frank Epperson. He loved playing around with flavors, but one chilly night, something surprising happened. Let's find out how little Frank's surprise turned into one of the most famous frozen snacks in the world!

Frank Epperson was born in 1894 in San Francisco, California, a city full of trolley cars, bustling markets, and salty ocean air. He was an inventive and curious kid. Whether it was recipes in the kitchen or building things with spare parts, Frank loved figuring out how things worked. His father worked as a real estate agent, but at home he encouraged Frank to explore and learn by doing. The kitchen became a mini science lab where Frank played with flavors, often creating his own drinks. One of his favorite things to make was homemade soda.

Back then, people often made their fizzy drinks at home by mixing flavored powder with water. This powder contained fruit flavoring, sugar, and citric acid to create the bubbly taste kids loved. It was cheaper than store-bought soda and allowed people like Frank to make their drinks just how they liked them: regular, extra sweet, or a little tart. Frank loved mixing different amounts of powder into his water to get the perfect bubbly beverage.

One night in 1905, eleven-year-old Frank was stirring a glass of his favorite homemade soda with a wooden stick. Without thinking much of it, he left it outside overnight. When he woke up the next morning and stepped onto the porch, he saw something strange. His drink had frozen solid! Then, when he grabbed the wooden stick to check on it, the entire frozen block came out in one piece. Curious, he took a bite. Cold, crunchy, and fruity - it was delicious! He ran inside to show his family. Frank had just invented the first-ever Popsicle®, but he didn't know it quite yet.

After discovering his frozen drink on a stick, Frank started experimenting. What if he tried different flavors? What if he let them freeze longer? Could he make them even better? At first, he left drinks out on cold nights, checking them in the morning to see which ones froze best. But since he couldn't control the weather, he started using an icebox, the old-fashioned version of a refrigerator, to freeze his drinks whenever he wanted. One day, he brought his new frozen treats to share with neighborhood kids. They were a hit!

Word spread. Soon, kids started asking for them, and Frank realized he might have something special. By the time he was eighteen years old, Frank had perfected his recipe. He switched from soda powder to fresh fruit juices, which tasted even better. He also made sure to use stronger wooden sticks so the frozen treats wouldn't slip off while being eaten.

Then, he had a big idea: what if he started selling them? Frank had the chance to sell lemonade pops at a firemen's picnic in town. At first, people didn't know what to think - wait, *this is a stick with frozen lemonade on the end?* But after one taste, they were hooked. Frank sold dozens of his treats that day, and he knew he was onto something big.

Even though Frank had been making his frozen treats since he was eleven, he didn't make his invention official with a patent (a way to protect your idea from being used by others) until 1923, when he was 29 years old. He originally called them "Epsicles" – a combo of his last name and "icicle," but his kids had another idea. They thought "Popsicles" was more fun and catchy than "Epsicle." The name stuck! Frank quickly started selling his Popsicles at California amusement parks, fairs, and street markets. The next year, in 1925, he sold the idea to the Joe Lowe Company, which expanded Popsicles across the country. Soon, kids everywhere were enjoying cherry, orange, and grape-flavored Popsicles for just a nickel each. As Popsicles became more popular, new flavors and versions were created – twin-stick Popsicles so kids could share, Fudgsicles® for chocolate lovers, and Creamsicles® with creamy fillings.

Frank's invention came at just the right time. In the 1920s and 1930s, the way food was made and sold changed forever. Before then, most food had to be fresh, homemade, or sold by local shops. But as factories and recipes improved, food companies started mass-producing snacks, cookies, cereals, canned goods, and frozen foods. Popsicles fit perfectly into this new world of packaged food. Freezers were improving too. By the 1930s, more homes had freezers that could store frozen treats like Popsicles. And factories got better at freezing. Ice cream and frozen snacks could now be made faster and in larger amounts. Shipping frozen food became easier as companies built better trucks. Without all of these changes, Popsicles might never have become as big as they did! Popsicles became one of the first frozen treats sold nationwide, along with ice cream bars and frozen dinners.

Even though Frank eventually sold the business, he never forgot how his invention began with one simple test on a cold night in California. Today, the Popsicle brand sells two billion popsicles a year, and the treat that started with just a cup of flavored water is now a global favorite. Frank's story teaches us that big ideas can come from small experiments, and sometimes, just being curious can lead to an unexpected discovery, even if you're just a kid. You never know what will *stick*.

DISCUSSION GUIDE

Review Questions

1. What was Frank Epperson originally mixing when he accidentally created the Popsicle®?

2. Why did Frank's kids suggest calling his invention a Popsicle instead of an Epsicle?

3. Which changes in technology helped Popsicles become popular nationwide?

Discussion Questions

1. Frank Epperson didn't stop after his first frozen drink experiment - he kept improving it. Can you think of other famous

inventions that were improved over time?

2. How do you think packaging and shipping might continue to change in the future? How might that change which foods or products are popular?

3. Frank was only 11 when he made his discovery. What are some small ideas, projects, or hobbies that you've worked on that could turn into something bigger?

Project Idea:

DIY Layered Popsicles®. What You Need: Small paper cups, Popsicle® sticks, 2-3 different fruit juices, Freezer

INSTRUCTIONS:

1. Pour first juice layer into the cup (about 1/3 full). Freeze for 30-45 minutes until slushy.

2. Insert the Popsicle stick into the slushy layer so it stands up.

3. Add the second layer of a different juice. Freeze 30-45 minutes more.

4. Add the final layer and freeze completely (about 2 hours).

5. Peel off the cup or run under warm water to remove. Enjoy!

Bonus Ideas: Try rainbow layers! Add fruit pieces or yogurt!

CHAPTER 17

PHILO FARNSWORTH (1906-1971)

FARM TO TELEVISION

As a teenager, Philo Farnsworth got a crazy idea from the most unlikely place. Surrounded by endless fields of crops on his family's farm in Idaho, he kept thinking about how the lines of dirt and crops ran in neat rows. His mind began to race. He thought, "What if lines like this could be used to send pictures?" This simple view of plowed fields sparked the idea that led to one of the biggest inventions in history: television. Curious to learn how this idea took off? Read on!

Born into a Mormon family in a log cabin in Utah in 1906, Philo moved to the farm in Idaho in 1918. Philo was always curious about the way things worked on the farm. He took apart motors and put them back together. He fixed electrical wiring in their farmhouse. But it wasn't just about fixing things – Philo wanted to create new things. He had an inventive spirit that seemed to grow stronger every day.

At 14, while plowing the fields one day, Philo noticed the rows of dirt being turned over by the plow and saw how the plow slowly changed messy dirt into clean lines. The straight lines and patterns made him think of how images could be broken down line by line into tiny pieces and then put back together again. That was when the idea for electronic television struck him. Philo imagined that a picture could be captured and sent using electricity and then put back together on a screen in lines. This was the idea of a lifetime. Philo's journey to change the world with the television had begun, and he was only 14.

At age 15, in high school, Philo read science articles that gave him more ideas about how to make television possible. Philo was so sure that his idea would work that he began sketching out plans for a device that could send pictures using electrons. He called it an "image dissector," a fancy way of saying it could break down and send images electronically.

Philo built his own homemade lab in the attic of his house. There, he put together different gadgets and experimented with electricity, trying to bring his idea of electronic television to life. By the time he was 16, Philo had become so knowledgeable that his high school chemistry teacher, Mr. Tolman, was amazed. Philo even shared his sketches of the first television system with Mr. Tolman, explaining his idea of how images could be scanned in rows, just like those fields he'd seen.

By the time he was 19, Philo had a working model for the first electronic television. Shortly after he moved to California with his new wife, his high school sweetheart, Pem Gardner, he made the first television. At just 21, Philo sent his first live image to a TV screen! It was just a simple line. It wasn't much, but it was the start of something that would change all of our lives.

Philo is not as famous as some other inventors, such as Alexander Graham Bell. When people think of early television, they often think of early TV makers and broadcasts. Americans have all heard of RCA and ABC, two early companies that made money off of TV, but many do not know Philo, who did not get rich from his idea. Maybe because he was more of an inventor than a businessperson? This biography is a good lesson about history and how the most important stories are not always about the most famous people.

But now *you* know about the farm boy who dreamed of sending pictures because of fields in Idaho. Philo's story shows that even the simplest observations – the simplest lives – can inspire incredible ideas. His early fascination with electricity and images became the building blocks for a technology that changed the world forever. Who knows what kind of discoveries you could make just by looking at the world around you?

Discussion Guide

Review Questions:

   1. What two states did Philo grow up in?

   2. What did he see in his everyday life that gave him the idea for sending and receiving pictures in lines?

   3. Who helped him work on his television invention?

Discussion Questions:

   1. Look at the inventions around you. Were these items brand new ideas or improvements on things that already existed? Any guesses about what might have led to the biggest ideas?

   2. Did television solve an everyday problem? Is inventing always about solving a problem or just making life more enjoyable? Or both?

   3. Why do you think Philo isn't better remembered for his world-changing invention?

Project Idea:

Create an Invention. Think like an inventor. Choose a problem in your everyday life and come up with an invention that solves it. Sketch out the idea or build a model using household and craft materials. Write a short description of how it works and explain why it's needed. Afterward, present the invention to classmates or family, just like Philo Farnsworth shared his vision for television.

PART VI

☆ ☆ ☆

BREAKING DOWN BARRIERS IN THE LATE 1800s AND EARLY 1900s

CHAPTER 18

HELEN KELLER (1880-1968)

THE YOUNG CHAMPION FOR PEOPLE WITH DISABILITIES

*B*efore she was even two years old, Helen Keller got very sick and was left both blind and deaf. Suddenly, the world she had begun to explore became black and noiseless. Each day was filled with anger and confusion. Her family was heartbroken. But somehow, with the help of a very special teacher, Helen eventually broke through the darkness and silence. She went on to become a famous fighter for the rights of those with special needs. This is Helen's incredible story.

Helen Keller was born on June 27, 1880, in Tuscumbia, Alabama. She was a bright and healthy baby. Her early life was filled with the usual joys and discoveries of childhood. At 19 months old, she became seriously ill, likely with either scarlet fever or meningitis. The illness took both her sight and hearing. Her parents didn't know how to deal with this new reality, and they struggled to raise Helen.

Without her eyes and ears, Helen at first couldn't communicate. If she were hungry or thirsty or tired or just wanted her doll, she couldn't tell anyone. The frustration of not being able to express herself led to tantrums. She would often lash out, throwing things and screaming.

Her family tried their best to understand her needs, but it was very hard. Helen's parents, especially her mom, refused to give up hope. They looked for advice from experts and eventually contacted Alexander Graham Bell, the famous inventor whose story is also in this very same book! Alexander suggested they reach out to the Perkins Institution for the Blind in Massachusetts. This connection would change Helen's life forever.

When Helen was six, a young teacher named Anne Sullivan arrived at the Keller family home. Anne had her own challenges. She had poor vision due to an infection in her childhood. But she was determined to help Helen. Anne used new methods to teach Helen how to communicate. Anne used a technique called "touch teaching," where she would spell words into Helen's hand with sign language to explain the world around her.

Of course, Helen didn't understand the touches right away. The breakthrough moment came one day when Anne took Helen to a water pump. She placed Helen's hand under the flowing water and spelled out "w-a-t-e-r" in Helen's other hand. Suddenly, Helen understood! She realized that the motions Anne was making matched the cool liquid flowing over her hand. Finally, Helen could connect with the world around her!

This "touch teaching" method opened up a new way for Helen to learn and communicate. Anne's patience and persistence were key. She worked tirelessly, day in and day out, to help Helen understand the world. Helen was very smart. She then learned to read and write using Braille, a writing system with letters you can feel. She even learned to speak, though that was a long process. Anne remained by Helen's side as her teacher and companion for many years. Their bond was unbreakable.

Despite Helen's challenges, even as a teenager she was determined to get the best education. She became the first deaf-blind person to earn a college degree, graduating from highly regarded Radcliffe College in 1904. Helen's success in college was not just a personal victory. It was a powerful message to the world that people with disabilities could achieve great things.

She used her education to fight for others. Helen wrote books and gave lectures, sharing her experiences and pushing for the rights of people with special needs. She also supported women's suffrage (the right to vote) and labor rights. Helen's story moved people then just as it moves you today – she had just done so much with so little, and she became famous. She used her fame to travel all over the world, speaking out for equal opportunity for all.

Helen Keller's work was part of the larger movements for disability rights and women's rights. At the time, people with special needs faced discrimination, but Helen's successes helped change the way the public saw people like her. She showed that with proper support, people with disabilities could lead full and productive lives. This movement continued successfully in the 20th century, with supporters pushing for access to education, jobs and even public buildings. Helen helped make a start for future progress.

Women's suffrage was also a major issue during Helen's lifetime. Women fought for the right to vote, which they got in 1920. Once again, Helen's accomplishments were simply impossible to ignore, and she helped women gain equal treatment under the law. Helen's life was an important part of these bigger struggles for equality.

Helen's story is a powerful reminder of what one brave person can do. Think about just going through an ordinary day without the ability to see or hear. Helen did so much *more* than ordinary things despite her challenges. She showed that no matter the vast obstacles, you can reach your goals, and that all started with the huge breakthroughs she made when she was just a child.

DISCUSSION GUIDE

Review Questions:

1. What was the first word Helen understood on her hand?

2. Where did she attend college?

3. What rights did she fight for in addition to rights for those with special needs?

Discussion Questions:

1. How do you think Helen's parents stayed strong after their daughter lost her sight and hearing?

2. What would your family do today if they needed help with something really important like the Kellers did when they found Anne Sullivan? Where would your family turn for help?

3. Why do you think Helen and Anne stayed together for so long?

4. Have you ever struggled to communicate something because of language or other obstacles? How did it feel? How did you overcome the challenge?

Project Idea:

Learning basic sign language can help you understand the importance of communication for people with disabilities. Sign language is a way of communicating using hand gestures, facial expressions, and body language. Many deaf and hard-of-hearing people use it to communicate. This activity will help you appreciate Helen Keller's story of overcoming communication barriers. It sounds hard, but I bet that you will surprise yourself and that this will be rewarding.

MATERIALS NEEDED:

- Sign language alphabet chart (can be found online)

- Paper and pen or markers

INSTRUCTIONS:

- Try spelling out your name using the sign language alphabet.

- Learn some basic words and practice them, such as "hello," "thank you," and "please."

- Practice signing with a family member or friend and write out the letters and phrases as you go.

CHAPTER 19

NEWSBOYS AND LOUIS "KID BLINK" BALLETTI (1881-1913)

KIDS FIGHTING FOR FAIRNESS

More than 100 years ago, in the bustling streets of New York City, kids as young as ten had to work hard just to earn a few pennies. These kids, known as newsies, sold newspapers on crowded corners, shouting the latest headlines to make a sale. But when the powerful newspaper owners tried to make life harder by raising prices, the newsies decided to fight back! Led by a brave and clever kid named Kid Blink, these young boys — and girls, too —made a stand that would echo through history.

The newsies were an essential part of city life. Every morning, they would wake up early, buy stacks of newspapers from the publishers for one price and then sell them for a little more to make money. The money they earned helped support their families. Newsboys were a familiar sight in big cities. They wore tattered clothes. Many were immigrants or the children of immigrants, families that had come to America in growing numbers.

In July 1899, the newsboys faced a big problem. Major newspaper publishers like William Randolph Hearst and Joseph Pulitzer increased the prices they charged the newsboys for their papers. The higher prices meant that the newsboys had to sell more papers to make the same amount of money. This was especially hard since many newsboys were already struggling. The increase felt unfair and hurt their ability to support their families. The boys decided they had to do something. They couldn't just accept this new price.

The newsboys organized a strike, which meant that they all got together and promised each other they would stop buying and selling papers. They refused to sell Hearst's Evening Journal and Pulitzer's New York World, the two largest newspapers at the time. They demanded that the publishers lower the prices back to what they were before.

The strike began in Long Island City and quickly spread to all parts of New York City. Soon, newsboys in other cities, such as Cincinnati and Nashville, joined the strike. The boys held meetings and formed a union, a group that promised to stand together and work only when the owners treated everyone in the union fairly. They chose leaders and planned their actions. One of the most notable leaders was Louis "Kid

Blink" Balletti, a charming teenager with an eye patch. Kid Blink became the face of the strike. His speeches and leadership inspired the other newsboys to stand strong.

The strike took work. The newsboys held rallies and marched through the streets, chanting and holding signs. They fought with police and strikebreakers who were hired to sell papers in their place. They armed themselves with sticks and stones.

The biggest newspapers refused to write stories about the strike. But other papers covered the events, quoting the newsboys in their excited way of talking. Kid Blink said: "Ain't that 10 cents worth as much to us as it is to . . . [the] millionaires? . . . If they can't spare it, how can we??" The boys' cause gained support from the public, who saw their struggle as a fight for fairness.

The strike lasted for two weeks and had a significant impact. Sales of the Evening Journal and New York World dropped by 20 percent. This loss hurt the publishers' pocketbooks. The boys' determination paid off. On August 1, 1899, the publishers agreed to a deal. They didn't lower the price, but they agreed to buy back any unsold papers from the newsboys each day. This new rule made a big difference to the newsies. It meant the boys wouldn't lose money on unsold papers or have to work around the clock to sell all the papers they had. The strike ended, but its effects lasted much longer.

The Newsboys' Strike of 1899 was a turning point in labor history. The strike led to changes in newspaper return policies. It showed the need for fair labor practices, especially for children, and it showed the power that kids could have if they stuck together. Today, laws govern when and how children can work. The strike was also part of a larger wave of labor movements during the 1890s. This period saw growth in cities and increased immigration, foreigners moving to America. Many people came to the United States seeking better opportunities. Cities like New York were growing fast. Immigrants brought diverse cultures and skills and helped growth, but they also faced challenges, including poor working conditions and low wages. The newsboys, many of whom were immigrants, were part of this changing city setting.

Their strike was not just about the price of newspapers. It was about fighting for their rights and improving their lives. The Newsboys' Strike of 1899 is a powerful example of how young people can make a difference – no matter how small you might feel, you have the power to stand up for what's right, especially if you and many others stand as one.

DISCUSSION GUIDE

Review Questions:

1. What was one of the newspapers the newsies refused to sell?

2. What cities besides New York had strikes?

3. True or false: the biggest papers wrote about the strike.

Discussion Questions:

1. Why do you think the newsies decided to make a stand? Why did they care so much?

2. Why do you think some of the newspapers refused to write stories about the newsies? Why did some papers choose to?

3. How does forming a union, an official group of workers who act together, help the newsies in their fight for fairness? How might the group not work for some individual news-boys?

Project Idea:

Create a Strike Poster. Creating a strike poster can help you understand the newsboys' fight for fairness. Use materials like paper, markers, and stickers to design a poster that captures the spirit of the Newsboys' Strike of 1899. Think about a message the newsboys wanted to say and how they could inspire others to back them up. Think about being bold and eye-catching. Share your poster with family and friends and tell the story behind the Newsboys' Strike of 1899.

CHAPTER 20

LOUIS ARMSTRONG (1901-1971)

BRINGING JAZZ TO NEW EARS

*I*t was New Year's Eve 1912 in the streets of a tough New Orleans neighborhood known as "The Battlefield." Eleven-year-old Louis Armstrong got ahold of his stepfather's gun and fired it into the night air of the celebration. That act of mischief got Louis sent to a home for troubled boys. Some might have thought that would be the end of his story. But it was in that home that Louis discovered the cornet, a brass musical instrument like a trumpet. Louis and the cornet were a match made in heaven. That was just the beginning of his story as a famous musician.

Louis was born on August 4, 1901, in New Orleans, Louisiana. From an early age, Louis faced many challenges. His family was very poor. To help his family, Louis did odd jobs, even as a young boy. He sold newspapers, delivered coal, and collected junk to sell. Despite these tough times, Louis found joy in music. He sang on the streets with a group of friends and even formed a boys' quartet. Singing was an escape, a way to find happiness.

Louis's love for music took off when he was sent to a reform school at age 11 after getting in trouble for firing a pistol. At the Waifs Home, he was introduced to the cornet, and everything changed. He practiced day and night, and before long, his incredible talent started to shine. He became the leader of the Waifs Home band. This early experience with music gave Louis a sense of purpose and direction. He realized that music could be his path out of hard times.

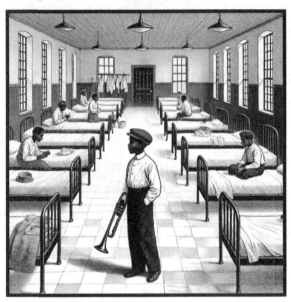

As a teenager, Louis was already known in New Orleans for his cornet skills. At 14, he was discovered by the jazz great, Joe "King" Oliver, who saw something special in Louis and became a mentor, like a coach. Louis even started earning money as a musician. At 16, he played with Fletcher Henderson's band. At 17, he showed his talent to larger crowds in parades with the King of Zulu. Just a boy, Louis was getting chances to learn from incredible jazz greats in the New Orleans scene.

Louis Armstrong's big break came when he was just 20 years old, and King Oliver invited him to Chicago to join his famous band, the King Oliver's Creole Jazz Band. This was a major turning point for Louis! In Chicago, he really blossomed as a musician. People were amazed by his powerful playing and his ability to create unique melodies on the spot. His fame quickly spread, making him a star in Chicago and later in New York.

The 1920s was known as the Jazz Age, a time when music in America changed in a big way. Before jazz, most music followed European traditions, but jazz brought something new and exciting. It blended African rhythms, blues, and ragtime to create a sound that was lively, unpredictable, and full of feeling. Musicians used jazz to express themselves in ways never heard before. It didn't just change music—it became a symbol of freedom and creativity in America.

Louis was at the center of this movement. His incredible talent and unique style actually helped jazz spread across the country. He knew how to put on a show. Audiences found his deep, scratchy voice, catchy smile, and playfulness on stage unforgettable. Just listen to him sing once. You won't forget it. Louis won the hearts of crowds everywhere. His recordings with the Hot Five and Hot Seven during the mid-1920s are considered some of the most important recordings in jazz history, showing his rare mix of instrument skill and emotion sharing. Louis also made popular recordings you'd probably recognize even today, such as his singing of *What a Wonderful World* – no one had a voice like Louis Armstrong.

Louis changed the way people thought about jazz. He made scat singing popular, where singers use silly syllables to sound like instruments. This fun, creative style added a new layer to jazz vocals. But his influence didn't stop at jazz; he became a symbol of new art and cultural change, bringing people together across different backgrounds and breaking down barriers as one of the first African American artists to gain wide fame.

Today, Louis Armstrong's legacy continues through the many musicians he inspired and the lasting popularity of jazz. The major airport in New Orleans is named for him! His life shows us that music can lift and connect all kinds of people. No matter how tough things get, there's always beauty and joy to find, just like Louis did in his incredible journey that started as a kid with a cornet.

DISCUSSION GUIDE

Review Questions:

    1. How did the boy's home change Louis's life?

    2. Who took Louis under his wing? How was that important in Louis's life?

    3. Name two cities he called home.

    4. When was the Jazz Age?

Discussion Questions:

    1. Can you think of other kinds of art besides jazz that are

based on totally free expression or creating something on the spot? Why do you think these arts have appeal to an audience? To a performer?

2. Why do you think that so much musical innovation (new ideas) came from America?

3. Can you think of examples of music bringing different people together?

Project Ideas:

1. **Create a Jazz Playlist**. Creating a jazz playlist can help you explore the rich world of jazz music and understand Louis Armstrong's influence. Choose a mix of classic jazz tunes and modern interpretations to appreciate the genre's diversity.

Access a music streaming service or a collection of jazz CDs. Start with some of Louis Armstrong's most famous recordings, like "What a Wonderful World," "Mack the Knife," and "West End Blues."

Add songs from other jazz legends like Duke Ellington, Ella Fitzgerald, and Miles Davis. Include modern jazz artists to see how the genre has evolved.

Listen to your playlist and pay attention to the different instruments, rhythms, and styles.

2. **Have a Scat Session.** A jazz music session with Louis Armstrong often included scatting, where Louis would use nonsense syllables, for example, "shoo ba dee do wop do," to copy the sound of a jazz instrument.

Find some clips of scat performers such as Louis (available online), then have kids pick their favorite current upbeat song and scat along to the melody. It's o.k. if you don't know the words – that's the whole point!

This jazzy activity will help you understand the freedom of the music and the expression of Louis Armstrong.

PART VII

☆ ☆ ☆

FIGHTING FOR FREEDOM IN THE MIDDLE 1900s

CHAPTER 21

AUDIE MURPHY (1925-1971)

ACTION-HERO SOLDIER

*O*n a cold winter day in France in 1945, a 19-year-old Texas farm boy found himself in a terrifying situation during the Second World War. He was surrounded by hundreds of enemy German soldiers and their tanks. He told his men to go back to save themselves. But he didn't go back. What happened next made this boy a legend. Read on to learn more about Audie Murphy.

☆ ☆ ☆

Born on June 20, 1925, in Kingston, Texas, Audie grew up during the Great Depression. This was a tough time for many families. Jobs were hard to find, and money was tight. Audie was the seventh of 12 children! From a young age, he had to help support his family. He picked cotton and did other farm work to earn money. These hard times shaped Audie into a tough young man, the kind of guy you'd want on your side in a fight.

When World War II began, Audie felt a strong duty to serve his country. He saw the military as a way to help his family and escape the poverty of his childhood. He tried to join the Marines and the Air Force but was turned down because he was too small. He was only 5 feet 5 inches tall and weighed just 112 pounds. Audie finally managed to join the Army in 1942 when he was just 17 years old. He had to lie about his age to get in. Audie did not know how to give up.

As it turns out, this small Texan packed a big punch. Audie fought in Europe against Nazi Germany. One of the key battles he fought in was the Battle of Colmar Pocket. On January 26, 1945, in the north of France, Audie's company was attacked by six German tanks and hundreds of enemy soldiers. Audie ordered his men to retreat - to fall back - to safety while he stayed behind to fend off the attackers. He climbed onto a damaged tank destroyer, which is like a small, quick tank. The destroyer was on fire and could have exploded at any moment, but Audie used its machine gun to hold off the enemy as they tried to close in all around him. Despite being wounded in the leg, Audie continued to fire for over an hour. This gritty little soldier was like a movie hero brought to life. His actions saved many lives and turned the tide of the battle. For this incredible bravery, he was awarded the Medal of Honor, the highest military award for courage in the United States.

Audie's bravery didn't end at the Battle of Colmar Pocket. Another unforgettable moment in his service happened in southern France on

"Pillbox Hill." Audie and his men were creeping up the hillside when, suddenly, a German soldier seemed to give up, raising his hands as if to surrender. But it was a trick. Audie's best friend went forward, believing the surrender was real, and was shot and killed by hidden German soldiers.

Fueled by anger and heartbreak, Audie sprang into action. He grabbed a machine gun, charging forward and firing as he advanced alone. Audie took on several German teams with remarkable focus and courage, forcing them to retreat. By the end, he had silenced multiple machine-gun nests almost by himself. For this brave act, Audie earned the Distinguished Service Cross, one of the highest honors in the U.S. Army.

By the war's end, Audie had received more than 20 medals, including the Distinguished Service Cross, two Silver Stars and two Bronze Stars. His actions made him the most decorated American soldier of World War II. Audie's story was so inspiring that he even appeared on the cover of Life magazine. He was a national hero.

World War II lasted from 1939 to 1945. It started when Germany, led by Adolf Hitler, invaded Poland. This act of war led Britain and France to declare war on Germany. The conflict quickly spread, involving many countries around the world. The United States entered the war after the Japanese attack on Pearl Harbor on December 7, 1941. This event united the nation and led to the growth of the American military and new efforts to make weapons. World War II included many significant battles, such as D-Day in Europe and the Battle of Midway in the Pacific. These battles were crucial in the Allies' ultimate victory, led by the U.S., United Kingdom and Soviet Union, against the Axis powers, led by Germany and Japan.

The battles Audie Murphy fought in were part of the larger struggle to defeat Nazi Germany. The Battle of Colmar Pocket was important because it helped secure the Allies' move into Germany. The Allies were lucky to have a special young soldier like Audie with special courage. He was a long way from home but was a born fighter. Audie's actions in this battle and others contributed to the eventual victory in Europe.

World War II greatly impacted the world, leading to the defeat of dictators - rulers with too much power, and the establishment of the United Nations, a group of countries that agreed to talk things over before going to war. It also set the stage for the Cold War and the struggle for civil rights and freedom that would continue in the decades to come – we'll talk about those events later in this book!

When the Second World War ended, Audie faced the challenge of returning to normal life. Like many war veterans, he struggled with the bad memories and nightmares he got from the war. But Audie didn't let this stop him. He spoke openly about his struggles, helping people to understand how it was hard to come back from a war and to be aware of mental health issues in general.

Audie also found a new path in Hollywood. He starred in 44 movies, many of them Westerns and war movies. His most famous role was playing himself in the film about his life, *To Hell and Back*. He played the role when he was a grown-up, but the truth is that when it happened, he was really just a kid. His amazing story inspires soldiers to this day.

DISCUSSION GUIDE

Review Questions:

1. Where was Audie from? What made him tough even as a little boy?

2. How old was he when he joined the Army?

3. Where were the battles he fought in during World War II?

Discussion Questions:

1. Why do you think Audie was willing to lie about his age to join the Army?

2. Do you think that young people make good soldiers? Why or why not?

3. Do you think it was fair of the German soldier to pretend to surrender at Pillbox Hill?

Project Idea:

Design a Medal for Bravery. Creating a medal for bravery can help you understand the significance of Audie Murphy's achievements. Think about what qualities make someone brave and how you can show those qualities in a medal design. You'll need paper, markers or colored pencils, scissors, ribbon and tape, staplers or glue.

Instructions:

- Draw the shape of your medal on paper and cut it out. It can be a circle, star, or any shape you like.

- Decorate your medal with symbols that represent bravery, such as a shield or a star.

- Write a word or phrase that captures the spirit of bravery, like "Courage" or "Hero."

- Attach a ribbon to the top of the medal using glue. Pin your medal on yourself or someone else!

CHAPTER 22

RUBY BRIDGES (BORN 1954)

THE BRAVE FIRST GRADER

*T*hink back to the first time you went to a new school. Maybe it was kindergarten. Were you nervous? Did you wonder what your teacher would be like? The other kids? What about your desk? Now imagine walking into that new school all by yourself, surrounded by crowds of angry people who didn't want you there. That's what Ruby Bridges faced day after day in 1960. Ruby was the first African American child to attend an all-white elementary school in New Orleans, Louisiana. She didn't back down, even when it was scary, and because of her courage, more kids of all backgrounds could finally go to school together. Here's Ruby's story.

Ruby was born on September 8, 1954, in Tylertown, Mississippi. Her parents, Abon and Lucille Bridges, were sharecroppers, which means that they grew crops on land they did not own and used a share of the crops to pay rent for the land. They moved to New Orleans, Louisiana, when Ruby was two years old. Ruby grew up in a small house with her parents and siblings. Her early life was filled with the simple joys of childhood. Still, it was also marked by the harsh realities of segregation, a system that kept African Americans and whites separate in the South.

In 1954, the same year Ruby was born, the Supreme Court of the United States ruled in Brown v. Board of Education that segregation in public schools was against the law. This ruling was supposed to end segregation, but many southern states resisted. In 1960, a court ordered Louisiana to allow African Americans to attend schools that had been only for white students, to desegregate schools.

Ruby was old enough to go to school at that time, and her parents wanted her to have the best education possible. They decided to en-roll her in an all-white school. Ruby and five other African American children were picked to take a test to find out if they could attend the all-white William Frantz Elementary School. Ruby passed the exam. Her father was worried about her safety, but her mother believed it was important for Ruby to have better opportunities. Ruby's mom wanted Ruby to pave the way for other African American children. In the end, she was the only African American who chose to attend that year.

Ruby started first grade at William Frantz Elementary School on November 14, 1960. Federal marshals, who are like police officers, led her and her mother to school because of the angry crowds waiting for Ruby. People shouted, held signs, and even threw things at them. It was a frightening scene. Each day for the rest of that school year, Ruby was escorted by federal marshals.

Inside the school, things were not much better. Many parents withdrew their children because of Ruby's presence, and only one teacher, Mrs. Barbara Henry, was willing to teach Ruby. For an entire year, Ruby was the only student in her class!

Ruby's determination was extraordinary. She never missed a day of school. She showed remarkable courage, walking past angry mobs and sitting alone in an empty classroom. Her teacher, Mrs. Henry, made the classroom a safe place. Ruby did really well in school. Mrs. Henry supported her the whole year, and the two formed a close bond. Ruby successfully stood up for her right to an equal education.

The Civil Rights Movement was gaining momentum during this time as African Americans fought for equal rights everywhere: in schools, buses, restaurants, and voting. Martin Luther King, Jr., was leading non-violent protests across the South – sit-ins at segregated restaurant counters, marches to state capitals. Key events such as the Montgomery Bus Boycott in Alabama were already taking place – you may have already heard of Rosa Parks, who started that protest.

Ruby's act of courage fit into this larger history. Her actions opened doors for other African American children to attend integrated schools. Ruby's story became a symbol of courage. Norman Rockwell famously painted "The Problem We All Live With," showing Ruby's first day at school. This painting got the nation's attention. Over time, more African American students enrolled at William Frantz Elementary School. Ruby's town began to share the school equally among whites and African Americans.

Ruby later graduated from a desegregated high school and became a travel agent. She married and had four sons. Later in life, Ruby reconnected with her first teacher, Mrs. Henry, and the two began telling people about their story. Ruby wrote two books about her journey and received the Carter G. Woodson Book Award. Disney made a movie about her. In 1999 she founded The Ruby Bridges Foundation to promote tolerance and change through education. Her story remains a testament to the power of standing up for what is right, no matter how young you are.

DISCUSSION GUIDE:

Review Questions:

1. What was the name of the Supreme Court decision that opened schools to African Americans?

2. How many other students were in Ruby's first class?

3. Who painted a famous picture of Ruby? What was it called?

Discussion Questions:

1. Why do you think Ruby's parents wanted her to attend the all-white school? How do you think she felt?

2. Why do you think Mrs. Henry wanted to teach Ruby?

3. How do you think Ruby got comfortable going to the new school? How long do you think that took?

Project Ideas:

1. **Write a Letter to Ruby.** One way to engage with Ruby's story is to write a letter to her expressing gratitude for her bravery. Think about what it must have been like for her to walk through those angry crowds and sit alone in her classroom. What would you like to say to her? How has her story inspired you?

2. **Plan a School Improvement Project.** Identify an area in your school that could be improved, such as the playground, library, or classroom resources. Describe the current conditions and think about what changes could make it better. Create a plan by showing the steps needed to make the improvements. Include who you will need to talk to and what you might need. Present your plan to your classmates and teachers.

PART VIII

☆ ☆ ☆

KID WARRIORS OF THE COLD WAR

CHAPTER 23

KIDS AS COLD WAR SPIES

YOUNG INFORMANTS AND CODEBREAKERS

I magine a world where children were not just playing soccer or doing homework but were also acting as spies. This might sound like something out of a movie, but it really happened during the Cold War. The Cold War was a time of great tension between the United States and the Soviet Union. It wasn't a war with guns and battles. It was a war of ideas and secrets. Both sides tried to gather as much information – called intelligence – as they could about each other. This is where spies came in. They were the eyes and ears of their countries, gathering vital information that could change the course of history. And some of these spies were just kids.

The Cold War began after World War II ended in 1945 and lasted until the early 1990s. The United States and the Soviet Union were the two most powerful countries in the world. They had very different ideas about how to run their countries. The United States believed in freedom and democracy, where people vote for how they want to be led. The Soviet Union believed in communism, where the government controlled many aspects of life. This difference in beliefs led to a lot of mistrust and fear.

Each side thought the other was trying to take over the world. On the map, there was a line between the two sides called the Iron Curtain. It was an invisible line that divided the free countries of Western Europe from the communist countries in the east.

Each side created powerful intelligence agencies to keep an eye on each other. In the United States, it was the Central Intelligence Agency (CIA). In the Soviet Union, it was the KGB. These groups were responsible for gathering information and protecting their countries from threats. The CIA used many methods to gather information, including codebreakers and informants, people living on the other side that the CIA paid for help. Sometimes, even young people got involved in these dangerous activities. Below, we'll talk about kids who were codebreakers and kids who were informants.

One of the most fascinating aspects of the Cold War was the use of codebreakers. These people tried to figure out secret messages sent by the other side. Many of these codebreakers were young and incredibly smart. They used their skills to help their countries. Picture yourself solving puzzles, but now with someone else's life depending on it!

One famous project was the Venona project. Starting in 1943, the United States tried to break the Soviet Union's secret codes to find out what the Soviet spies were doing. Many of the American decoders were young women, such as Angeline Nanni from Pennsylvania, who were really good at math or languages. Angeline was just 16 when she started work as a codebreaker. She and other young puzzle solvers played a big role in discovering who the Soviet spies were in America.

Young informants also played a crucial role during the Cold War. These were young people who provided important information to intelligence agencies. They often found themselves in the middle of dangerous situations. One amazing case was during the Cuban Missile Crisis in 1962. This was a time when the United States and the Soviet Union came very close to starting a nuclear war. The Soviet Union had put nuclear missiles on the island of Cuba, just 90 miles from Florida in the United States. The world was on the brink of disaster.

The Cuban youth informants involved during the Cuban Missile Crisis were teenagers, about 14 to 18 years old. They weren't Americans – at least not yet – but they helped the American side. They saw things adults didn't see. These kids were often outside during the day while adults were at work. The teens were on foot instead of in cars, so they noticed things you might not see while driving fast down a road. The kids also spent more time hanging out and talking to other kids, so they shared a lot of information with each other. For these reasons, the young Cubans were valuable informants. They bravely told American spies what they saw of Soviet military work in Cuba. They helped the U.S. avoid nuclear war!

The Cold War was fought with information and secrets. Kids were able to help. After all, kids are sometimes able to do things that adults can't. When was the last time you saw a grown-up play hide-and-go-seek or climb over a fence? By breaking codes and gathering information, brave kids helped the U.S. win the Cold War.

DISCUSSION GUIDE

Review Questions:

1. Who fought in the Cold War?

2. What did the two different sides of the Cold War believe in?

3. What made kids good informants in Cuba during the Cuban Missile Crisis?

Discussion Questions:

1. Do you think including kids in spying during the Cold War was fair? Why or why not?

2. Why do you think it was so important to break the Soviet

codes? What would happen if they didn't?

3. Do you think being a spy is more or less dangerous than being a normal soldier?

Project Idea:

Spy Scavenger Hunt. Pretend to be a spy with this fun scavenger hunt. Go to a public place and find different characteristics of people without being caught. For example, look for someone with brown hair, someone wearing blue jeans, or someone carrying a red bag. Try to do this without letting anyone know you're watching them. This activity will help you understand the importance of observation and secrecy in espionage.

CHAPTER 24

JOAN BAEZ (BORN 1941)

THE GIRL WHO SANG FOR CHANGE

I magine a summer night, the ocean breeze, and an outdoor concert with thousands of people there to hear America's best folk musicians. A little-known teenage girl steps onto the stage, her long, dark hair shimmering in the lights. She starts strumming her guitar and sings with a voice so clear and beautiful that everyone stops breathing just to listen... She becomes a star almost overnight. That's how Joan Baez burst onto the national folk-music scene at the Newport, Rhode Island, Folk Festival in 1959 when she was only 18. How did she get there, and where did it take her?

☆ ☆ ☆

Joan Chandos Baez was born in 1941, on Staten Island in New York, into a family that valued education, compassion, and activism. Her father, a physicist and inventor, worked on projects that took the family across the globe, including Baghdad, Iraq. Experiencing so many different cultures shaped Joan's understanding of the world and inspired her sense of justice.

As a child, Joan didn't immediately stand out as a musician — she even admitted she wasn't the best at practicing her violin! But everything changed when she discovered folk music as a teenager. Folk songs were simple yet powerful, telling stories of ordinary people and their struggles.

Joan taught herself to play the guitar and the folk music she loved. Her father's work brought the family to Cambridge, Massachusetts, where the large population of students helped make the area a hotbed of young folk performers. A teenage student herself, Joan did informal performances at first, then had regular gigs (shows that paid) at coffeehouses around Cambridge and Boston. Her unique voice and emotional delivery quickly set her apart, earning her some local fans, and Joan began playing at clubs, cool places like Club 47.

Joan's big chance came at that 1959 Newport Folk Festival when she was 18. Bob Gibson, a well-known folk singer at the time, invited her to join him on stage as a guest performer. Gibson had noticed her talent in the Boston folk scene and thought her voice would grab the festival audience. He introduced her to the crowd, and when Joan stepped onto the stage, she sang two duets with him, including "Virgin Mary Had One Son."

The audience was blown away by her pure, haunting voice. This special moment quickly turned Joan into a sensation (someone whose fame was growing fast). Different recording companies wanted her. She signed with Vanguard Records because of their promise to stay true to folk. Before she even turned 20 years old, she released her first album, Joan Baez, featuring old ballads and spirituals like "House of the Rising Sun" and "Henry Martin." She quickly became one of the leading voices in the folk music revival.

But Joan wasn't just singing to entertain. Her performances were often tied to important causes. She marched with Martin Luther King Jr. during the Civil Rights Movement and inspired protesters with songs like "Oh Freedom." She made a stance against the Vietnam War, which was a conflict in Southeast Asia where U.S. forces tried to keep South Vietnam independent. Many Americans did not think it was worth the risk for American soldiers to fight there. To protest the war, Joan often performed a song at rallies, "Where Have All the Flowers Gone?" Joan used her fame to amplify (make louder) the voices of those fighting for justice, whether on a stage at Carnegie Hall or singing outside on the steps of the Lincoln Memorial in Washington, D.C.

Joan rose to fame during the golden age of folk music in the 1960s. Rock' n' roll radio stations jokingly refer to those years as "the folk scare" because folk was nearly as popular as rock 'n' roll. Folk music became well-liked because it told real stories, often with themes of justice, love, and community. It was also easy to play and sing along to, making it the perfect soundtrack for protests and rallies and the clubs, coffeehouses and parties where youth gathered. Artists like Pete Seeger, Woody Guthrie, and Bob Dylan were among Joan's peers, and together, they gave folk music a new energy. Songs like Dylan's "The Times They Are A-Changin'," which Joan frequently performed, became anthems for the movements of the time.

The 1960s were turbulent years. Folk music provided a voice for people who wanted to speak out. Joan was at the center of it all, her voice soaring over marches and gatherings, bringing people together. She was a different kind of Cold War warrior – she was a warrior for peace.

DISCUSSION GUIDE

Review Questions:

1. What type of music did Joan Baez sing to inspire people and fight for change?

2. At what famous festival did Joan Baez perform when she was just 18 years old, making her an overnight star?

3. Can you name other famous folk singers mentioned?

Discussion Questions:

1. Do you think Joan would have been as famous if she had not

had the chance to sing at the Newport Festival? Why or why not?

2. Why do you think Joan Baez used her voice and music to stand up for fairness and peace? How can art and music make a difference in the world today?

3. Why was folk music often the music of 1960s protests? What is it about folk music that worked well with 1960s youth movements?

Project Ideas:

1. **Design a Concert Poster**: Pretend Joan Baez is performing in your town during her early career. Design a colorful, eye-catching concert poster with the name of the event, songs she might sing, and why the concert matters.

2. **Write a Mini Biography Comic Strip**: Turn art into a story by making Joan Baez's biography into a comic strip. Illustrate key moments from her life, like performing at the Newport Folk Festival or marching for civil rights. Add speech bubbles to show her inspiring words.

CHAPTER 25

1980 USA MEN'S HOCKEY TEAM

OLYMPIC MIRACLE

F ive... four... three... the entire stadium was going crazy as the time counted down. The TV announcer, Al Michaels, yelled what every American felt: "Do you believe in miracles?! Yes!" It was 1980 at the Winter Olympics in Lake Placid, New York. A group of young American hockey players had created a moment that would be remembered forever. Known as the "Miracle on Ice," these Americans came together to do the impossible – they beat the Soviet Union's hockey team. The Soviets were supposed to be the most incredible team on the planet. The U.S. team was just a bunch of kids. The American victory was not just a triumph on the ice, but a win that lifted an entire nation. Here's the unbelievable true story.

The tale of this incredible team began with a group of college players from all over the United States. They were not paid athletes; they were just college students who played hockey for the love of the game. The USA players were all young men, mostly around 20 years old. The youngest player on the team was Mike Ramsey, who was only 19 years old at the time of the Winter Olympics. Despite his young age, Mike was in the starting lineup on defense because he was a great skater who could also help on offense. He would go on to have a great professional career after the Olympics.

The American team was coached by Herb Brooks, a man with a clear plan for victory. Coach Brooks believed in these young players and pushed them to do their very best and then to go even further! He knew that to beat the Soviet team, they would need more than just skill. They would need stamina (the ability to keep playing without getting tired), heart and trust in each other.

The Soviet team, on the other hand, was a powerhouse. They had won the last four Olympic gold medals in hockey and had not lost an Olympic game in 12 years. Their team was made up of experienced professionals – paid players – who had played together for years. They were fast, skilled, and tough. They had the best support staff. Most thought they would skate their way to the gold medal again.

The plan for the U.S. team was simple but challenging. Coach Brooks knew that they couldn't win with just better skills and shooting. Instead, they needed to outwork the Soviets and use every small chance they got. The game plan focused on fast skating, tight defense, and quick tries to score. The players needed to stick to the plan no matter what.

Every practice, they tried to build their toughness and teamwork to prepare them for the fast speed of the Soviet game.

When the game against the Soviet Union finally took place, both teams were undefeated – they had won or tied every game – so far in the Olympics. Everyone was tense in the stadium. The whole world was watching.

The Soviets scored first. But the American team quickly answered. Neither team would let up. They skated hard. They hit harder. Both teams fought for every loose puck. As the time ticked off in the first period, the U.S. made a long shot on the Soviet goalie to get the puck into the Soviet end. It was an easy save for the Soviet goalie. But then the rebound split two Soviets, and American Mark Johnson skated in fast. He quickly gathered the puck and moved in on the Soviet goalie. He made a hard move to his left and scored! Just past the Soviet goalie's kicked-out leg. And just as the first period ended. That made it 2-2 with two periods to go. This was a sign that it might be the USA's game. The Americans started to believe.

After the Soviets took a 3-2 lead in the second period, the USA tied the game in the third and final period. Then, with about eight minutes to go, Mike Eruzione got the puck in the Soviet end. He moved across the ice in front of the goal. Before anyone could stop him, he fired a quick shot past a defender. The puck beat the Soviet goalie under his arm! Goal! The team crowded Mike in celebration. The Americans had the lead, 4-3!

The final moments of the game were a test of energy and willpower. The Soviet team wouldn't stop attacking, but the American defense, led by goalie, Jim Craig, held firm. Jim made a bunch of big saves, keeping the lead and finally getting the victory. As the final buzzer sounded, the American players burst with joy, knowing they had achieved something extraordinary—a miracle! They went on to win the gold medal.

The "Miracle on Ice" took place against the backdrop of a tense Cold War. In 1980, the world was split. Some countries were on the side of the United States and democracy, where people voted for the leaders and laws they wanted. Other countries were on the side of the Soviet Union and communism, where government controls more of what people do and say.

Also, the Soviet Army had invaded the smaller country of Afghanistan in late 1979, and many people in the U.S. were angry. In fact, the U.S. refused to go to the 1980 Summer Olympics in the Soviet Union because of the war in Afghanistan. This refusal to participate is called a boycott, a form of protest.

The relationship between America and the Soviet Union was not good. In addition to the Cold War with the Soviets, the U.S. was dealing with other problems at home, including high prices of gas and groceries, and it was harder to find good jobs in 1980.

So the Olympic victory came in the middle of all of these challenges. It was more than just a hockey game. It changed the national mood in the U.S. It showed Americans that if they worked together, they could win the Cold War. It showed them that they had the spirit and ability to beat the odds, to fix their problems. All that happened because a bunch of kids did the impossible in a hockey game.

DISCUSSION GUIDE

Review Questions:

1. Where were the 1980 Winter Olympics held?

2. Who was the youngest player on the U.S. team?

3. What was the final score of the game against the Soviets?

Discussion Questions:

1. How can sports help build unity among people?

2. What does the Miracle on Ice teach us about facing challenges that seem impossible? How did the coach and the team get the win?

3. Do you think that the team had a real impact on the Cold War? Why or why not?

Project Idea:

Mini Olympics. Host a mini "Olympics" with your friends. Pick which countries you want to play for. You can have floor hockey for the Winter Games and races for the Summer Games. This activity will help you understand the importance of teamwork and competition. Have fun, and see how working together makes you stronger!

As we've journeyed through the pages of this book together, we've also journeyed through American history.

Through Time. We've met remarkable young Americans across four centuries! From brave kids of the Colonies in the 1600s to the courageous youth of the Cold War in the 1980s, each story has shown us that age doesn't limit the ability to make a difference.

Through Perspectives. Each chapter has told us about young people from different backgrounds and regions of the country and kids who impacted history in different ways. We've explored the lives of children who fought for freedom and those who led the way west. We've seen how young inventors changed the world and how kids like Helen Keller and Louis Armstrong broke down barriers. We've delved into the stories of young civil rights activists, spies and even heroic hockey players.

Through Events. You also now know about many meaningful periods in American history: the Colonies, the Revolution, the frontier, the Civil War, the Industrial Age, the Jazz Age, the Second World War, the Civil

Rights Movement and the Cold War. You learned how those events were for kids like you. That means you understand those times better and how we got where we are today. You know what made America. And that helps you know what will shape her in the future.

Through Discussion. So take a moment to discuss what you've read. Talk with your family or friends about the stories you liked the most. Ask yourself questions: what would you have done in their place? How can you apply their bravery and determination to your own life? These discussions can help you understand the importance of these stories and how they relate to your own life.

Learning More. I encourage you to learn more too. The stories in this book are meant to be short and fun, but there is a lot more out there to read about all these heroes. Pick a couple favorites and go to the library for a longer biography!

Overall. Of the many lessons in this book, this one is probably the most powerful: you don't have to be a big deal to do something big. Through their bravery, creativity, and determination, these young people have changed American history.

I think they're so inspiring. If they've inspired you too, then think about how you want to shape your story. Find something you care about and get started. You could run for student council, volunteer at the local seniors center or sign up for guitar lessons.

Remember, many kids in this book worked at passions that lasted a lifetime, making bigger impacts later. Don't be afraid to find something you love to do right now. After all, these young people were just like you. They had dreams, faced challenges, and took action. You can too.

Final Note. One last thing about learning history and the times we live in. As I reflect on my years studying American history and raising a family, I realize that I appreciate today's world more because I understand the challenges of America's past. I appreciate my neighbors more because I know where we all came from. History is not just about *long ago*. We all make history every day. We're all part of the tale of this country. We're all in this together.

Thank you for joining me on this adventure! Keep learning, keep questioning and keep diving into whatever you're passionate about. America is waiting for your story!

MAKE HISTORY WITH YOUR REVIEW!

"A single act of kindness throws out roots in all directions, and the roots spring up and make new trees." – Amelia Earhart, American aviation pioneer

You've just read about some incredible real-life kids who changed American history. Now you have the chance to help someone else find these inspiring stories!

Most people decide what to read based on reviews.

That's where you come in!

> Your review could:
> ...help one more kid find his or her passion.
> ...help one more teacher find the perfect book for class.
> ...help one more family talk about a new story together.

It take less than a minute to leave a review; just scan this QR code:

Thank you sincerely for sharing the promise of kids and history!

N. H. Greenwood

REFERENCES IN ORDER OF USE

·Mary Chilton: The Young Mayflower Passenger. (n.d.). Mayflower 400 UK. Retrieved from https://www.mayflower400uk.org/education/who-were-the-pilgrims/2020/july/mary-chilton/

·Ann Putnam, Jr: Villain or Victim? (n.d.). History of Massachusetts Blog. Retrieved from https://history-ofmassachusetts.org/ann-putnam-jr/

·The Salem Witch Trials. (n.d.). Bill of Rights Institute. Retrieved from https://billofrightsinstitute.org/essays/the-salem-witch-trials

·Martin, J. P. (1830). Narrative of some of the adventures, dangers, and sufferings of a Revolutionary Soldier. Hallowell: Glazier, Masters & Co.

·Joseph Plumb Martin's Memoir. (n.d.). Museum of the American Revolution. Retrieved from https://www.amrevmuseum.org/collection/joseph-plumb-martin-s-memoir

·Peter Francisco: The Incredible Hulk of the Revolution. (n.d.). American Battlefield Trust. Retrieved from https://www.battlefields.org/learn/articles/peter-francisco

·Sybil Ludington. (n.d.). American Battlefield Trust. Retrieved from https://www.battlefields.org/learn/biographies/sybil-ludington#:~:text=Ludington%20made%20her%20ride%20on

·Wheatley, P. (n.d.). His Excellency General Washington. Retrieved from https://poets.org/poem/his-excellency-general-washington

·Phillis Wheatley. (n.d.). Britannica. Retrieved from https://www.britannica.com/biography/Phillis-Wheatley·Sacagawea. (n.d.). Britannica. Retrieved from https://www.britannica.com/biography/Sacagawea

·Fleming, T. (2013). A Disease in the Public Mind. De Capo Press.

·David G. Farragut. (n.d.). American Battlefield Trust. Retrieved from https://www.battlefields.org/learn/biographies/david-g-farragut

·Tucker, S. (2012). The encyclopedia of the War of 1812: A political, social, and military history. ABC-CLIO.

·Hearn, C. G. (2011). Admiral David Farragut: The Civil War years. Naval Institute Press.

·Mahan, A. T. (1892). Farragut. Little, Brown and Company.

·Crossing Wyoming: Kit Carson and a Changing West. (n.d.). Wyoming History. Retrieved from https://www.wyohistory.org/encyclopedia/crossing-wyoming-kit-carson-and-changing-west

·Sides, H. (2006). Blood and thunder: The epic story of Kit Carson and the conquest of the American West. Anchor Books.

·Carter, H. L. (1996). Kit Carson: Indian fighter or Indian killer?. University of Oklahoma Press.

·Lavender, D. (1972). Bent's Fort. University of Nebraska Press. (Original work published 1954)

·Olive Oatman. (n.d.). Mojave Desert. Retrieved from http://mojavedesert.net/people/oatman.html

·John Clem. (n.d.). American Battlefield Trust. Retrieved from https://www.battlefields.org/learn/biogra-phies/john-clem#:~:text=Rather%20than%20surrender%2C%20Clem%20shot

·Axelrod, A. (2007). The horrid pit: The Battle of the Crater, the Civil War's cruelest mission. Carroll & Graf Publishers.

·Reid, W. (1868). Ohio in the war: Her statesmen, her generals, and soldiers. Moore, Wilstach & Baldwin.

·McFeely, W. S. (1991). Frederick Douglass. W. W. Norton & Company.

·Fought, L. (2017). Women in the world of Frederick Douglass. Oxford University Press.

·Quarles, B. (1968). Frederick Douglass: An American slave. University of Michigan Press.

·Douglass, F. (2003). Narrative of the life and works of Frederick Douglass. Bedford/St. Martin's. (Reprint edition)

·Black Soldiers in the Civil War. (n.d.). National Archives. Retrieved from https://www.archives.gov/edu-cation/lessons/blacks-civil-war/douglass-sons.html

·George Westinghouse. (n.d.). Britannica. Retrieved from https://www.britannica.com/biogra-phy/George-Westinghouse

·Alexander Graham Bell: Inventor of the Telephone. (n.d.). Ducksters. Retrieved from https://www.duck-sters.com/biography/alexander_graham_bell.php

·The Invention of the Telephone. (n.d.). Clemson University. Retrieved from https://opentextbooks.clem-son.edu/sciencetechnologyandsociety/chapter/the-invention-of-the-telephone/

·Industrial Revolution. (n.d.). History.com. Retrieved from https://www.history.com/topics/industrial-rev-olution/industrial-revolution

·Epperson, F. (1923). Epsicle patent application. U.S. Patent No. 1,505,592.

·Lowe, J. (1925). Acquisition of Epsicle Company. Business archives.

·National Museum of American History. (n.d.). The history of frozen treats in America. Smithsonian Institution. Retrieved from https://americanhistory.si.edu

·Popsicle Brand. (2022). Our history. Retrieved from https://www.popsicle.com

·San Francisco Historical Society. (2018). Early 1900s innovations from San Francisco. Bay Area Archives.

·Philo T. Farnsworth. (n.d.). Franklin Institute. Retrieved from https://www.fi.edu/hall-of-fame/phi-lo-t-farnsworth

·Philo T. Farnsworth and the Invention of Television. (n.d.). History Channel. Retrieved from https://www.history.com/topics/inventions/philo-t-farnsworth

·Allen, T. B. (2002). Farnsworth and the invention of television. Scholastic.

·The Philo T. Farnsworth Archives. (n.d.). Retrieved from https://philotfarnsworth.com/

·Newsboys on Strike. (1899, July 25). The Sun. Retrieved from https://cityhallpark1899.com/newspaper-articles/sun/july-25-1899a/

·Newsboys Strike in New York. (1899, July 18). Zinn Education Project. Retrieved from https://www.zinnedproject.org/news/tdih/newsboys-strike/

·Helen Keller Meets Anne Sullivan. (n.d.). History.com. Retrieved from https://www.history.com/this-day-in-history/helen-keller-meets-her-miracle-worker

·American Foundation for the Blind. (n.d.). Helen Keller biography and chronology. American Foundation for the Blind. https://www.afb.org/about-afb/history/helen-keller/biography-and-chronology/biography

·Biography.com Editors. (2021, January 21). Helen Keller - Family, quotes & teacher. Biography. https://www.biography.com/activists/helen-keller

·Louis   Armstrong.   (n.d.).   Britannica.   Retrieved from https://www.britannica.com/biography/Louis-Armstrong#:~:text=Early%20life%20and%20career,-Quick%20Facts&text=Although%20Armstrong%20claimed%20to%20be

·Louis Armstrong. (n.d.). Biography.com. Retrieved from https://www.biography.com/musician/louis-armstrong

·Teachout, T. (2009). Pops: A life of Louis Armstrong. Houghton Mifflin Harcourt.

·Immigration and Urbanization. (n.d.). Lumen Learning. Retrieved from https://courses.lumenlearning.com/suny-ushistory2ay/chapter/immigration-and-urbanization-2/

·Audie Murphy Single-Handedly Stopped a German Attack. (n.d.). National WWII Museum. Retrieved from https://www.nationalww2museum.org/war/articles/audie-murphy-single-handedly-stopped-german-attack

·Beevor, A. (2015). Ardennes 1944: The Battle of the Bulge. Penguin Books.

·Murphy, A. (1949). To hell and back. Henry Holt and Company.

·Ruby Bridges. (n.d.). National Women's History Museum. Retrieved from https://www.womenshistory.org/education-resources/biographies/ruby-bridges

·Cold War Spy Stories. (n.d.). Child's World. Retrieved from https://www.childsworld.com/shop/show/7636

·The Women Code Breakers Who Unmasked Soviet Spies. (n.d.). Smithsonian Magazine. Retrieved from https://www.smithsonianmag.com/history/women-code-breakers-unmasked-soviet-spies-180970034/

·The Cuban Missile Crisis, 1962. (n.d.). CIA. Retrieved from https://www.cia.gov/resources/csi/static/888b1a6acc282f122ec52b60c61bce99/Cuban-Missile-Crisis-1962-1.pdf

·Blight, J. G., & Welch, D. A. (1990). On the brink: Americans and Soviets reexamine the Cuban Missile Crisis. Hill and Wang.

·Baez, J. (1987). And a voice to sing with: A memoir. Summit Books.

·Smithsonian Folkways Recordings. (n.d.). Joan Baez. Retrieved from https://folkways.si.edu

·Hajdu, D. (2001). Positively 4th Street. Farrar, Straus and Giroux.

·U.S. Hockey Team Beats the Soviets in the "Miracle on Ice". (n.d.). History.com. Retrieved from https://www.history.com/this-day-in-history/u-s-hockey-team-makes-miracle-on-ice

·Mike Ramsey. (n.d.). USA Hockey Hall of Fame. Retrieved from https://www.ushockeyhallof-fame.com/page/show/830346-mike-ramsey

·Childhood Memories of the Cuban Missile Crisis. (n.d.). NPR. Retrieved from https://www.npr.org/2012/10/22/163395079/childhood-memories-of-the-cuban-missile-crisis

*Cover image "flag ribbon" designed by Freepik

Glossary

Abolition (U.S.): The movement to end slavery of African Americans, which was especially important during the 1800s, helping spark the American Civil War.

Allies (WWII): Countries, including the U.S., Britain, and the Soviet Union, that worked together to defeat the Axis Powers in World War II (1939–1945).

American Frontier: The expanding western edge of the United States during the 1800s, where settlers explored and built new communities.

American Revolution: The war fought by the American Colonies to gain independence from Britain (1775–1783).

Axis (WWII): The countries led by Germany, Italy, and Japan that fought against the Allies in World War II (1939–1945).

Battle of Yorktown (in American Revolution): The last major battle of the American Revolution at Yorktown, Virginia, where American and French forces defeated the British in 1781.

Braille: A system of raised dots that people who are blind or visually impaired can read with their fingers.

Brown vs. Board of Education (1954 Supreme Court Ruling): The court decision that said segregation in schools was unfair and illegal.

Central Intelligence Agency (CIA): The U.S. government agency responsible for gathering information and conducting secret missions to protect national security.

Civil Rights Movement: A struggle chiefly in the 1950s and 1960s to end unfair treatment of African Americans and to secure equal rights for all.

Civil War: A war fought between the Northern states (Union) and Southern states (Confederacy) over the South's trying to leave the U.S. due to wanting to maintain slavery (1861–1865).

Cold War: A long period of tension between the U.S. and the Soviet Union after World War II, without actual fighting (1947–1991).

Colonies (as in 13 Colonies): The first 13 areas settled by Europeans in North America under British rule. These later became the United States. They were Connecticut, Delaware, Georgia, Maryland, Massachusetts, New Hampshire, New Jersey, New York, North Carolina, Pennsylvania, Rhode Island, South Carolina and Virginia.

Communism: A system where the government owns businesses and property, makes most decisions without citizen input, and says it will share resources equally among the people.

Confederacy: The group of Southern states that separated from the U.S. during the Civil War.

Continental Army: The Army led by George Washington that fought for American independence during the American Revolution.

Cuban Missile Crisis: A tense event in 1962 when the U.S. and Soviet Union almost went to war over nuclear weapons in Cuba.

Democracy: A type of government where people vote to pick their leaders and make decisions.

Dylan, Bob: A famous singer and songwriter born in 1941 who became an important voice in the 1960s folk music movement.

Edison, Thomas: An inventor known for creating the light bulb, phonograph, and more (1847–1931).

Folklore: Traditional stories, songs, and customs passed down in a community.

Folk Music (1960s America): A type of music that uses simple melodies to tell stories, often passed along by word of mouth and shared across places and generations.

Fremont, John C.: An explorer, soldier, and politician who helped map the American West (1813–1890).

Fur Trade (in American West): The trapping, buying and selling of animal furs for clothing, which was a major business during the 1700s and 1800s.

Hearst, William Randolph (as Publisher): A famous newspaper publisher who created a large media empire including the *New York Journal*

(1863–1951).

Hidatsa Tribe: A Native American tribe known for farming and living in villages along the Missouri River.

Hollywood (Films): The center of the American movie business located in Southern California.

Industrial Age: A time during the 1700s and 1800s when machines were invented that changed how people worked and lived.

Informants (in Spying): People who secretly share information with intelligence agencies or police.

Intelligence (in Spying): The gathering of secret information about other countries, organizations, or people to learn their plans, strengths, or weaknesses. This information helps governments make decisions for national security.

Iron Curtain: The imaginary line dividing communist and democratic countries in Europe during the Cold War.

Jazz Age: A period in the 1920s when jazz music and dance became very popular.

Jefferson, Thomas: The third President of the United States and writer of the Declaration of Independence (1743–1826).

Justice (in Activism): Fair treatment and equal rights for all people, often fought for through protests or activism.

KGB: The Soviet Union's secret police and intelligence agency during the Cold War.

King, Martin Luther Jr.: A leader of the Civil Rights Movement who fought for equality through peaceful protests (1929–1968).

Lewis and Clark (Corps of Discovery): Explorers who led an expedition to map the Louisiana Territory (1804–1806).

Louisiana Territory: A large area of land purchased by the U.S. from France in 1803 that doubled the country's size.

Mass Production: Making lots of the same thing the same way in a factory so that many people can have it.

Mayflower (Ship): The ship that brought the Pilgrims to America in 1620.

Mayflower Compact: An agreement made by the Pilgrims to create fair laws for their new colony.

Mexican-American War: A war between the U.S. and Mexico over land in the West (1846–1848).

Militia (in American Revolution): Local groups of soldiers who fought for American independence.

Mohave Tribe: A Native American tribe from the southwestern United States known for farming and trade.

Mormons: Members of a religious group founded in the U.S. in the 1800s who moved west to practice their religion more freely.

Nazi Germany: The dictatorship led by Adolf Hitler during World War II (1933–1945).

New World: A name Europeans used for the Americas after their discovery.

Oliver, Joe "King": A famous jazz musician and bandleader who helped develop early jazz (1885–1938).

Parks, Rosa: A Civil Rights leader who refused to give up her bus seat to a white person, sparking protests (1913–2005).

Patent: A special rule that gives an inventor the right to be the only one to make and sell an idea.

Paul Revere's Ride: A midnight ride in 1775 to warn American colonists of a British attack.

Phonograph: A machine invented by Thomas Edison that could record and play sound.

Pilgrims (in Plymouth): A group of people who traveled to America in 1620 to find religious freedom.

Pioneer (in American West): A settler who moved west to start a new life on the frontier.

Plymouth Rock: The traditional landing spot of the Pilgrims in 1620.

Pulitzer, Joseph: A famous newspaper publisher who made the news exciting and started the Pulitzer Prizes for great writing and journalism. His big newspaper was the *New York World* (1847–1911).

Puritans: A group of religious people who came to America first in the 1600s to build communities based on their devout beliefs.

Salem Witch Trials: A series of trials in 1692 in Salem, Massachusetts, where people were accused of practicing witchcraft.

Sit-in Protest: A peaceful way to protest by sitting in a place and refusing to leave until rules are changed or unfairness recognized.

Scat (in Music): A style of singing in jazz where nonsense words or sounds are used instead of lyrics.

Segregation: The separation of people by race, which was protested during the Civil Rights Movement.

Shoshone Tribe: A Native American tribe living in the western United States, known for hunting and fishing and helping guide settlers and explorers such as Lewis and Clark.

Spy (in Espionage): Someone who secretly gathers information about other countries or organizations.

Steam Engine: A machine that heats water to make steam to create power, helping drive the Industrial Revolution.

Strike (in Labor): When workers stop working to protest unfair treatment or demand better pay for their work.

Telegraph: A machine that sends messages over long distances using electric signals sent as dots (shorter signals) and dashes (longer signals), which form a code called Morse code.

Union (Civil War): The group of Northern states that fought to keep the U.S. together during the Civil War.

Union (in Labor): A group of workers who join together to fight for fair treatment and pay.

Underground Railroad: A secret network that helped enslaved people escape to the North to be free.

Vietnam War: A war in Southeast Asia where the U.S. fought to stop the spread of communism (1955–1975).

Wampanoag Tribe: Native American tribe who lived in the area we now call Massachusetts and Rhode Island. They helped the Pilgrims survive when they arrived in 1620 by teaching them how to grow food and live off the land.

War of 1812: A war between the U.S. and Britain fought over disputed land in today's Midwest and the British blocking of U.S. sea trade (1812–1815).

Washington, George: The leader of the Continental Army during the American Revolution and the first President of the United States (1732–1799).

Wild West: A nickname for the western U.S. during the 1800s, known for cowboys, outlaws, and pioneers.

Women's Suffrage Movement: The fight for women to gain the right to vote, which succeeded in 1920 in the U.S.

World War I: A global conflict fought mainly in Europe between the Allies and Central Powers (1914–1918).

World War II: A global conflict between the Allies and Axis Powers (1939–1945).

Made in the USA
Monee, IL
06 April 2025

15052836R00094